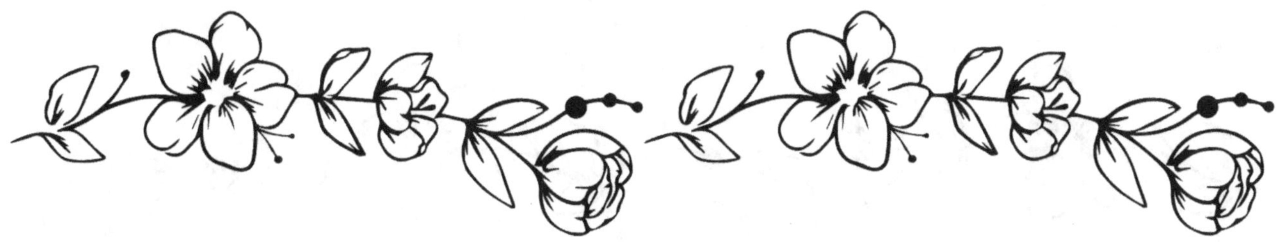

This Book Belongs to:

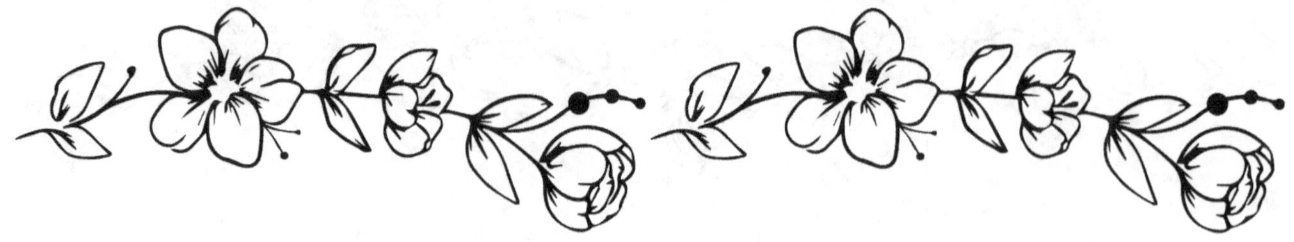

"WELCOME TO OUR SPRING-THEMED ADULT COLORING BOOK! EXPLORE THE BEAUTY OF THE SEASON WITH DETAILED DESIGNS READY TO BE FILLED IN WITH YOUR FAVORITE COLORS. IMMERSE YOURSELF IN THE SERENITY OF NATURE AND ENJOY THIS MOMENT OF CREATIVE RELAXATION WHILE CELEBRATING THE RENEWAL AND EXUBERANCE OF SPRING."

Leticia Seraphim

Test Color Page

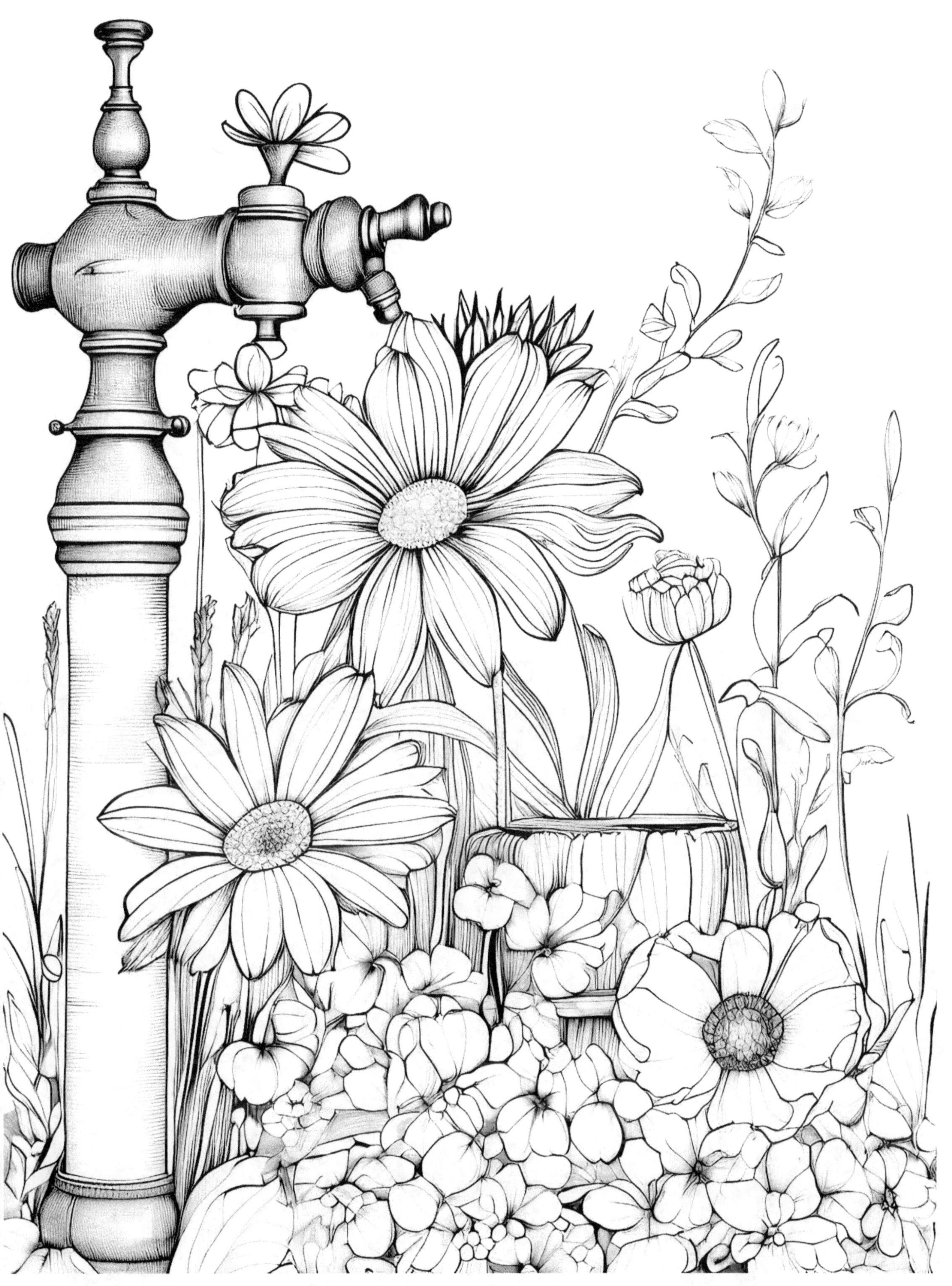

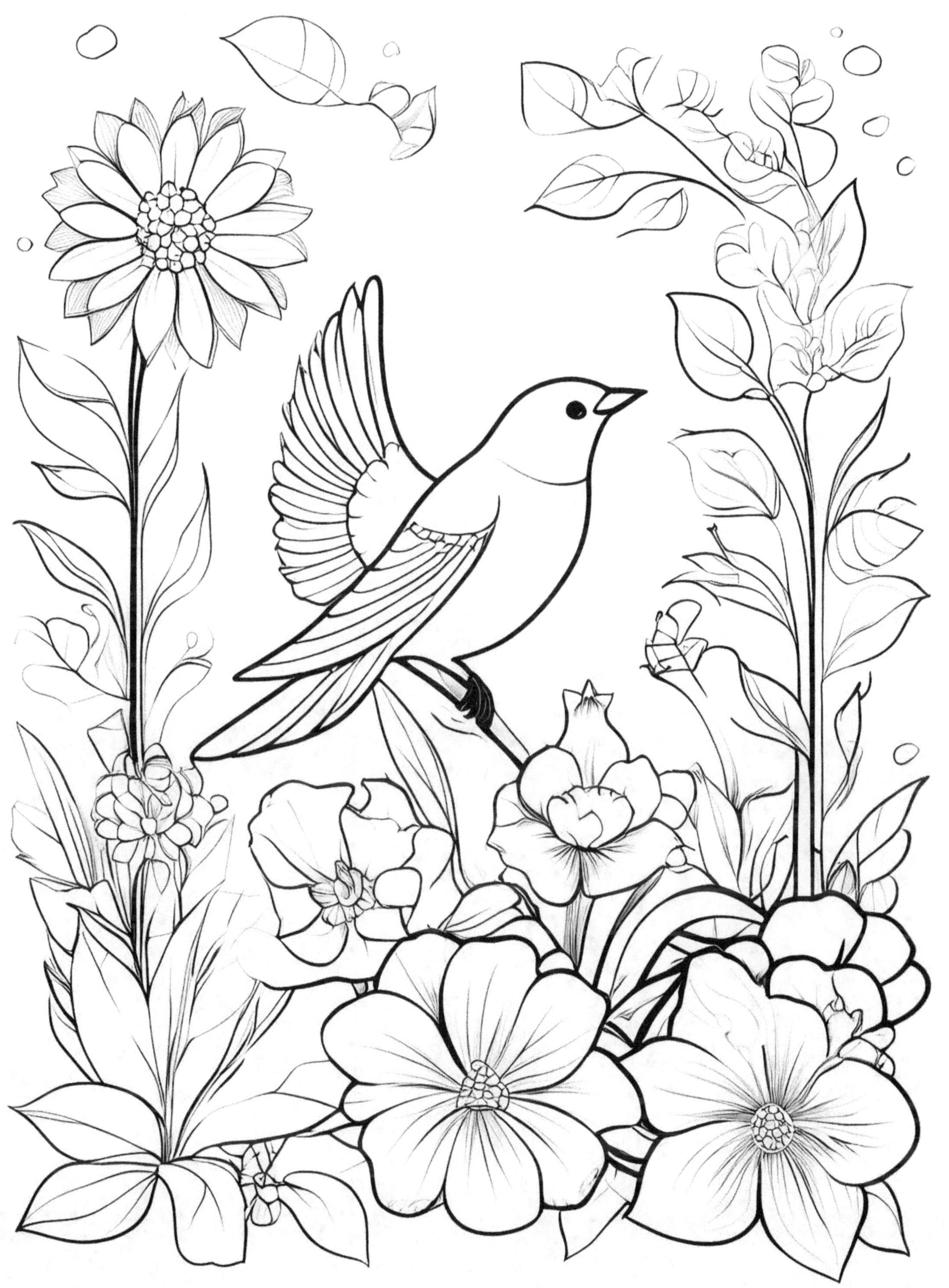

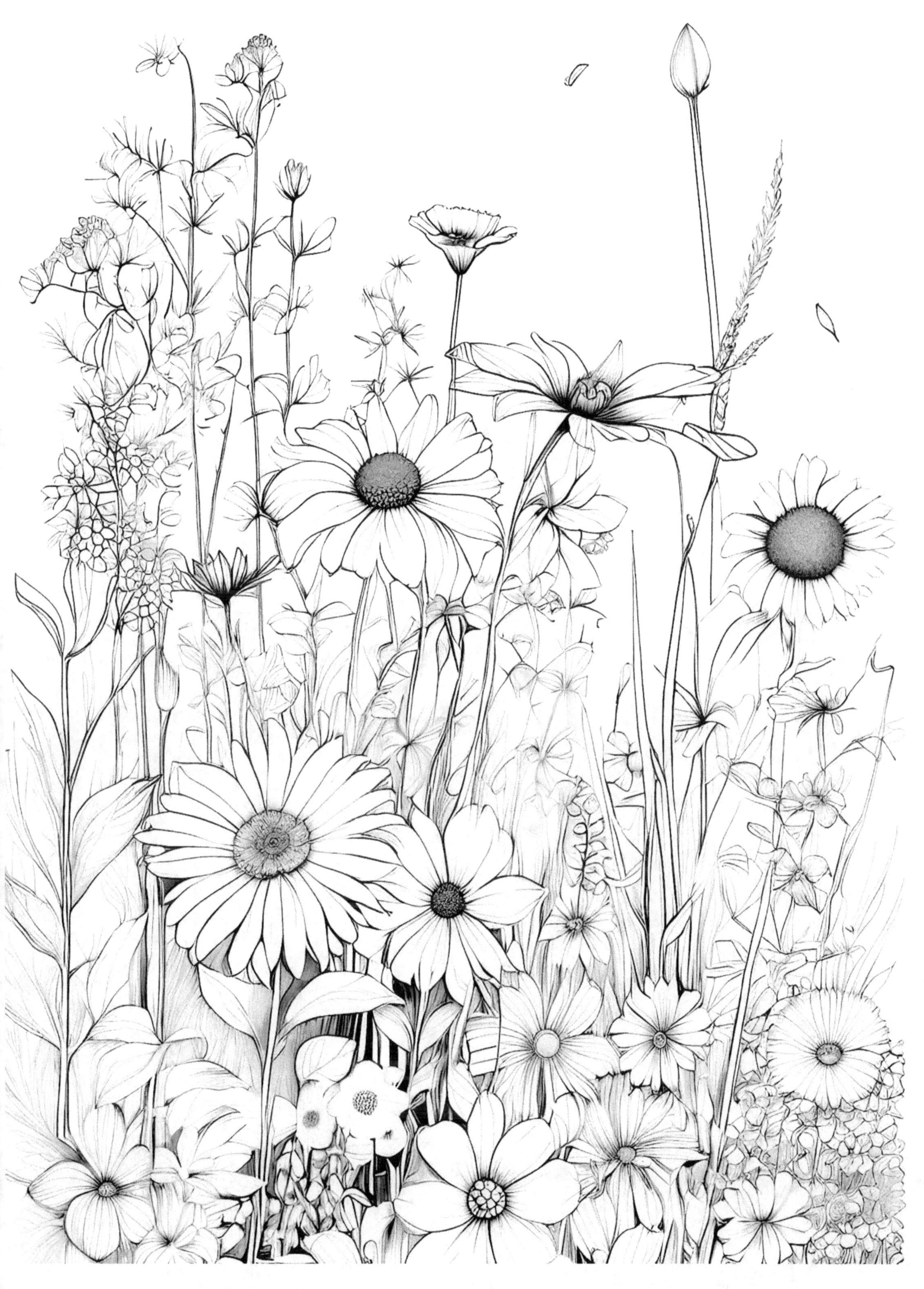

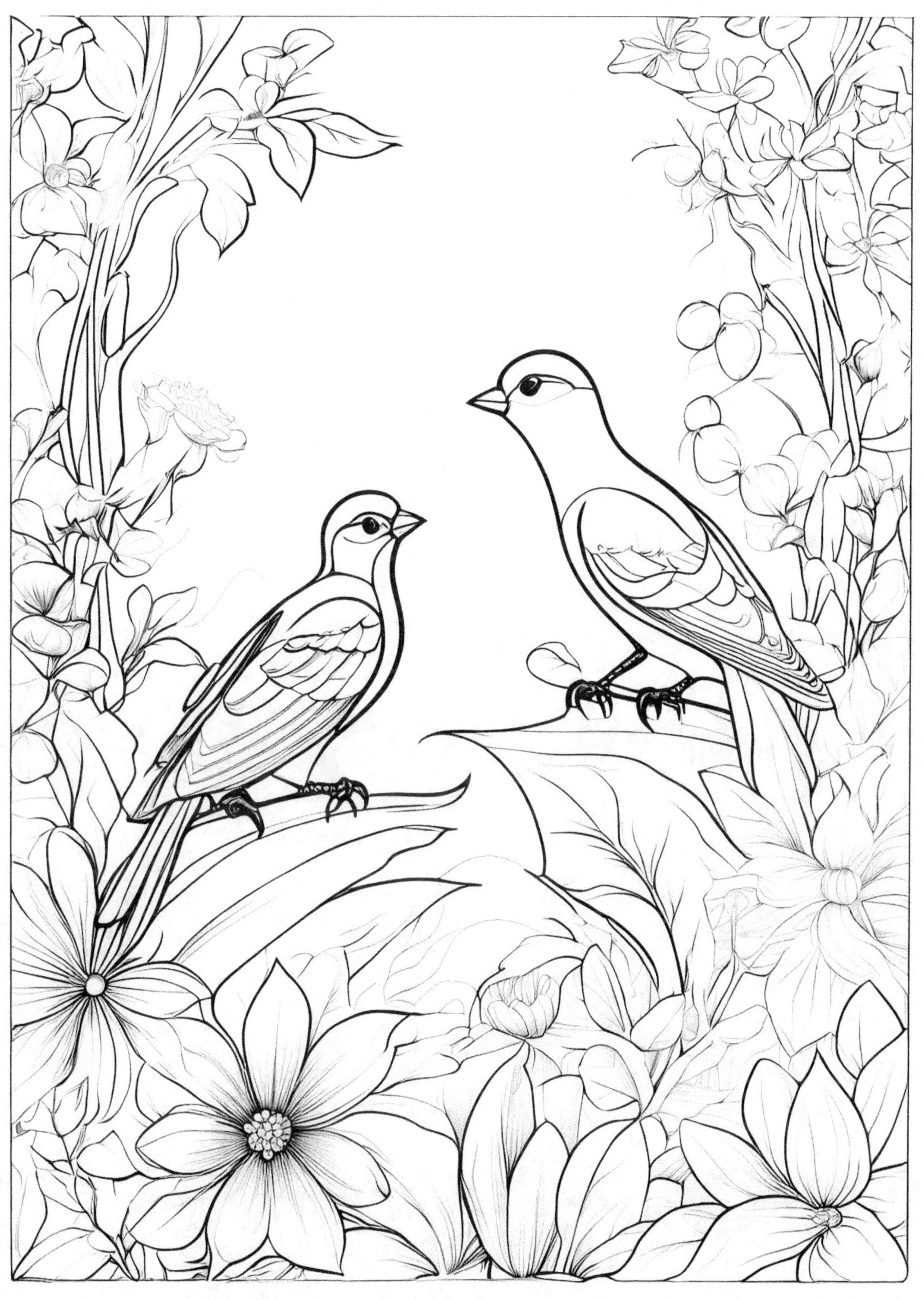

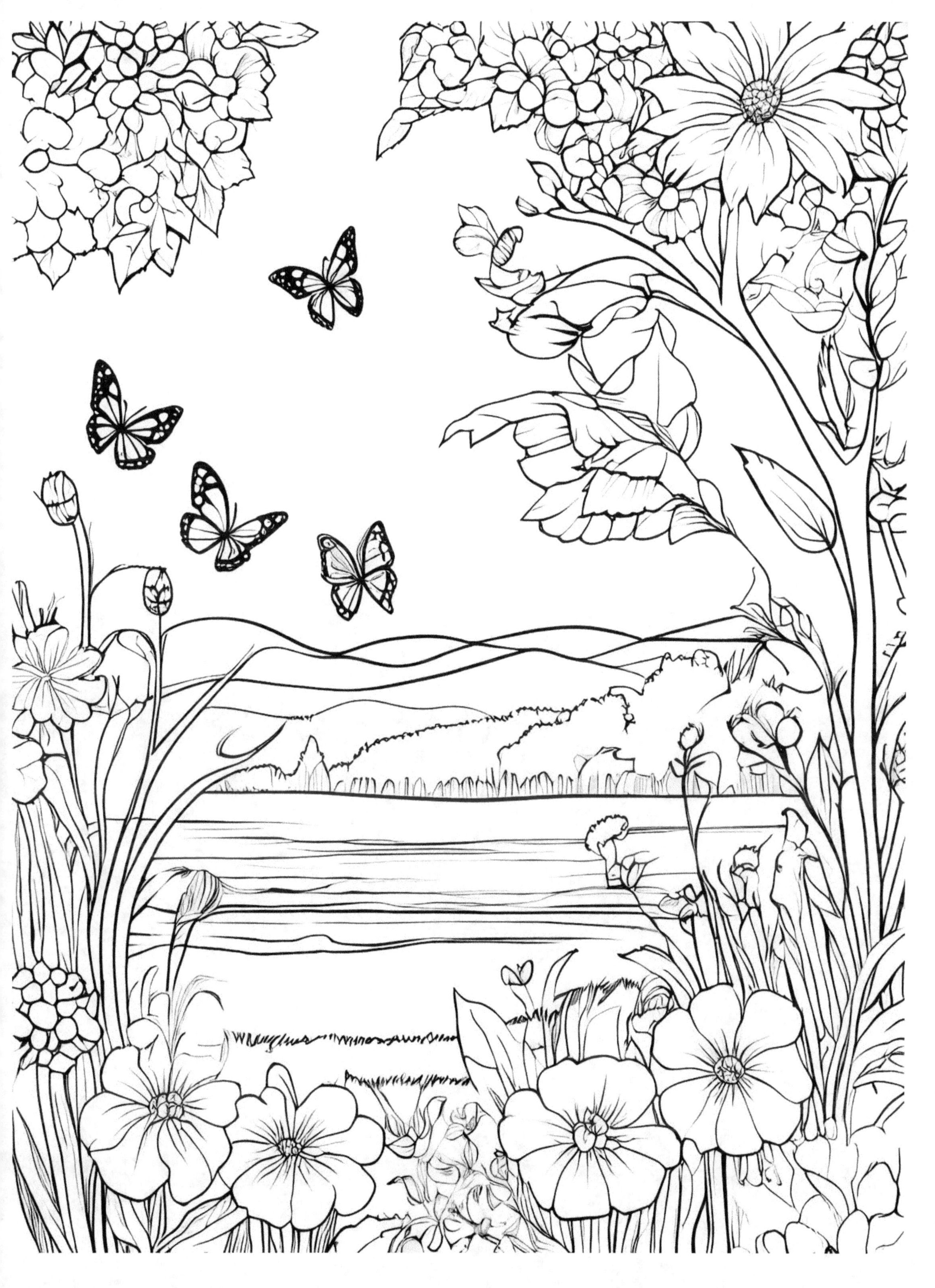

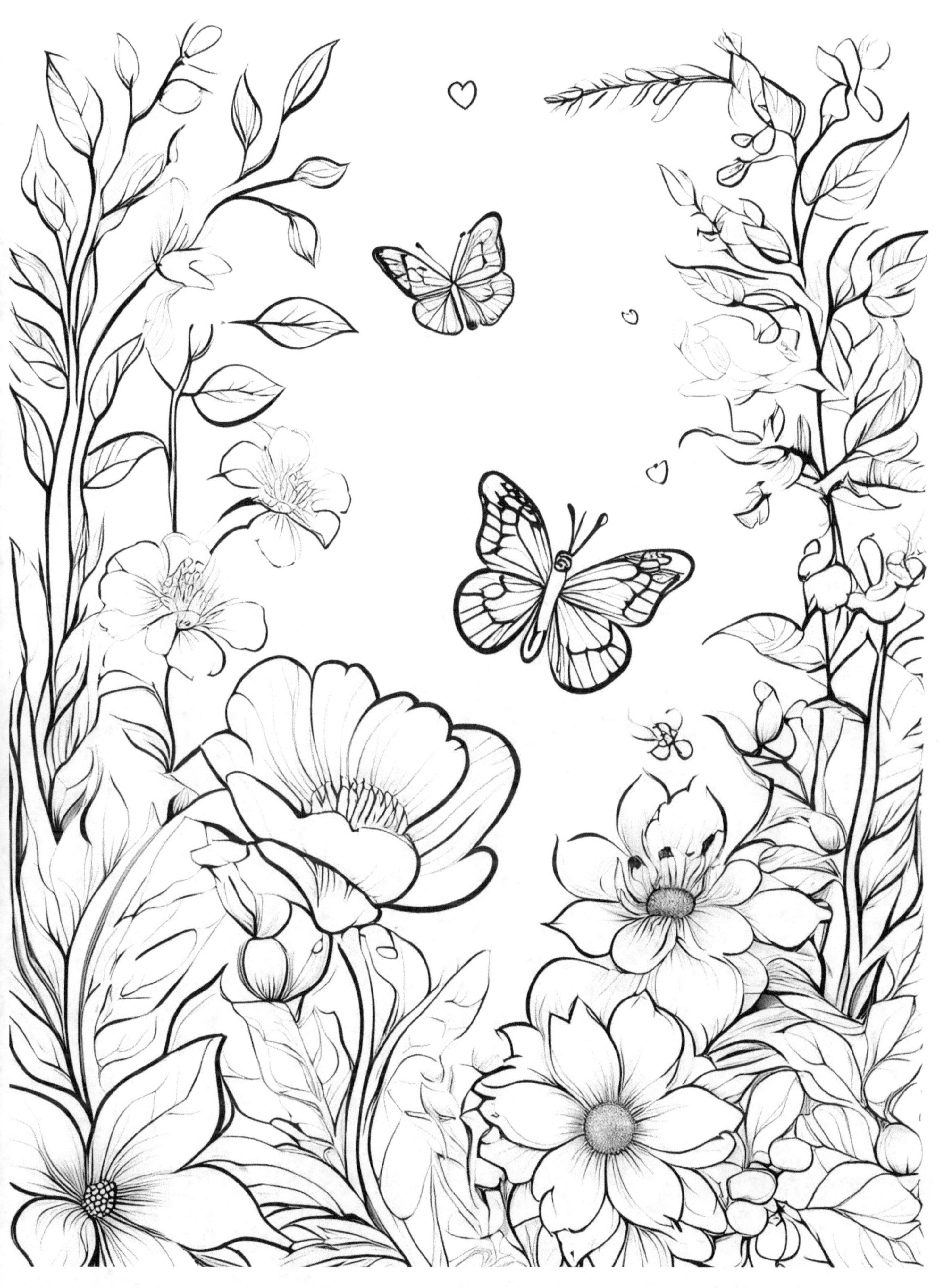

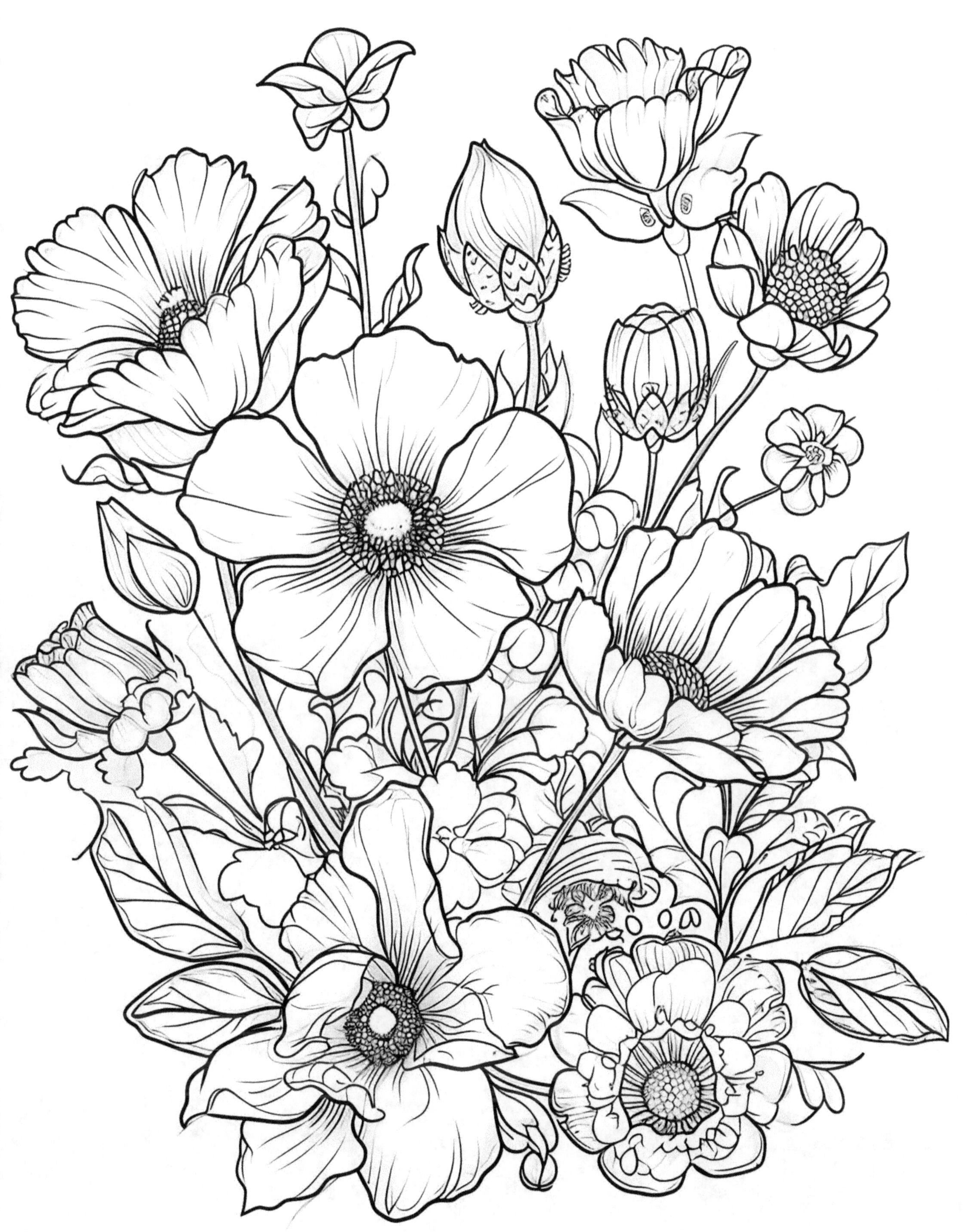

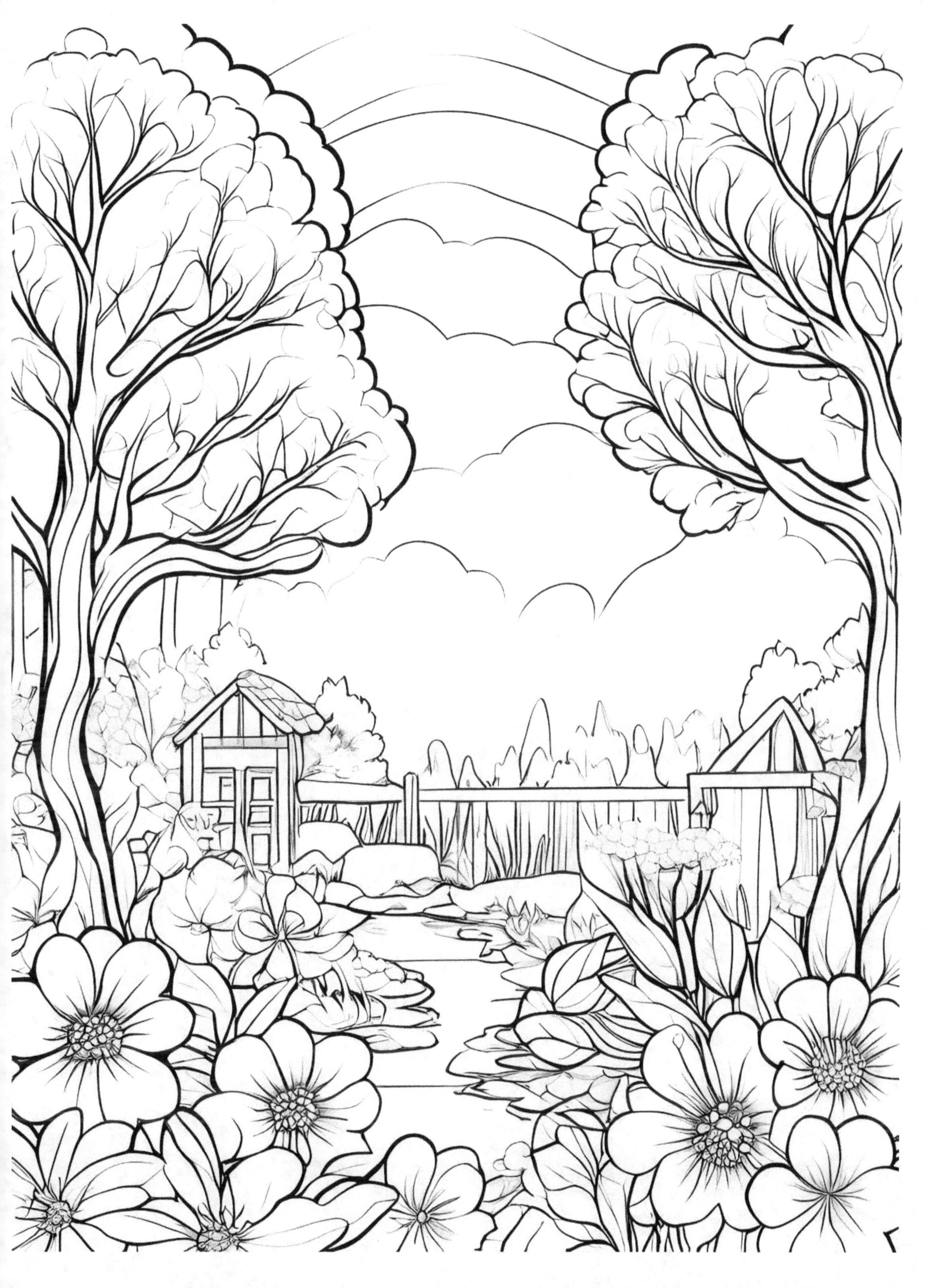

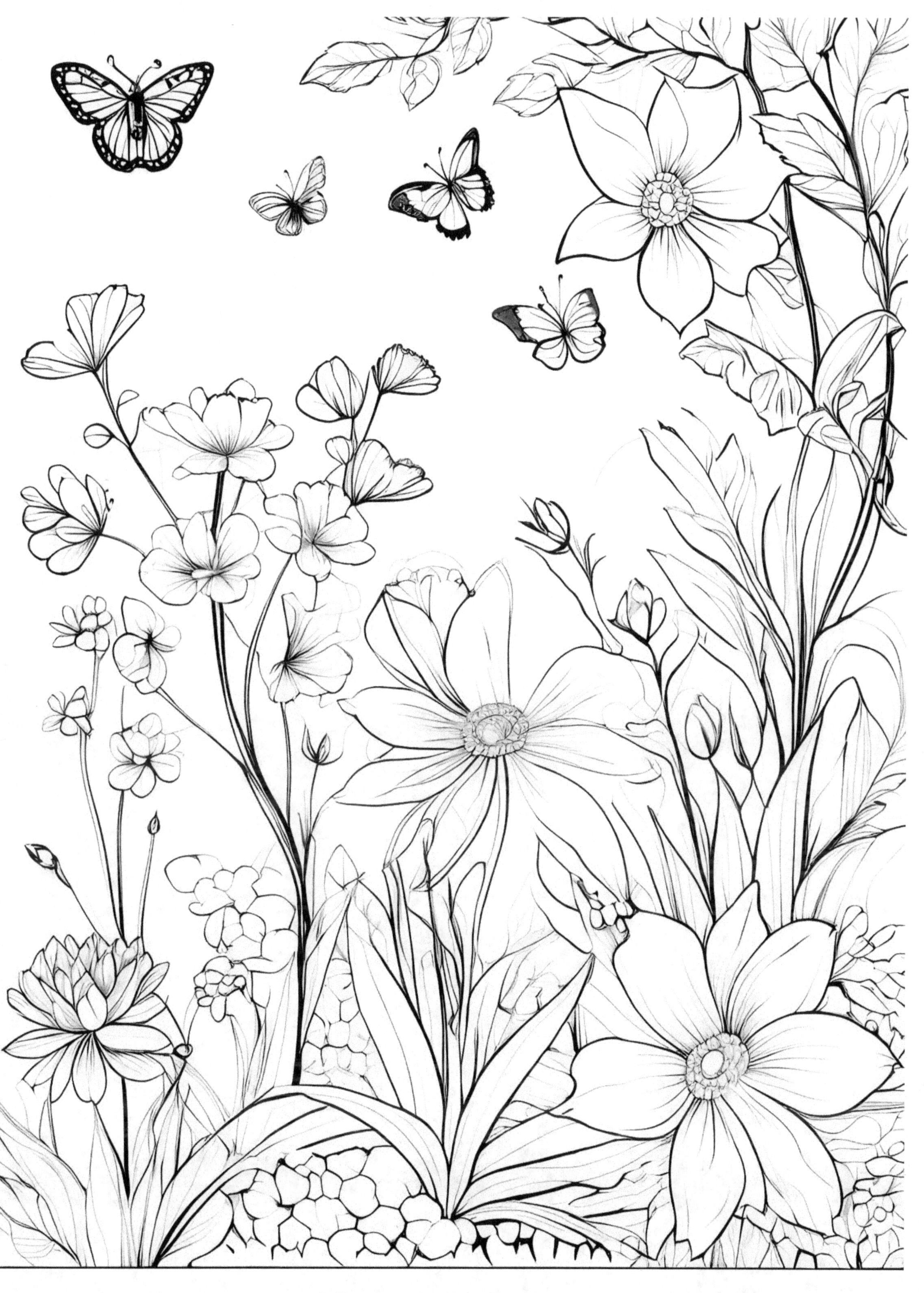

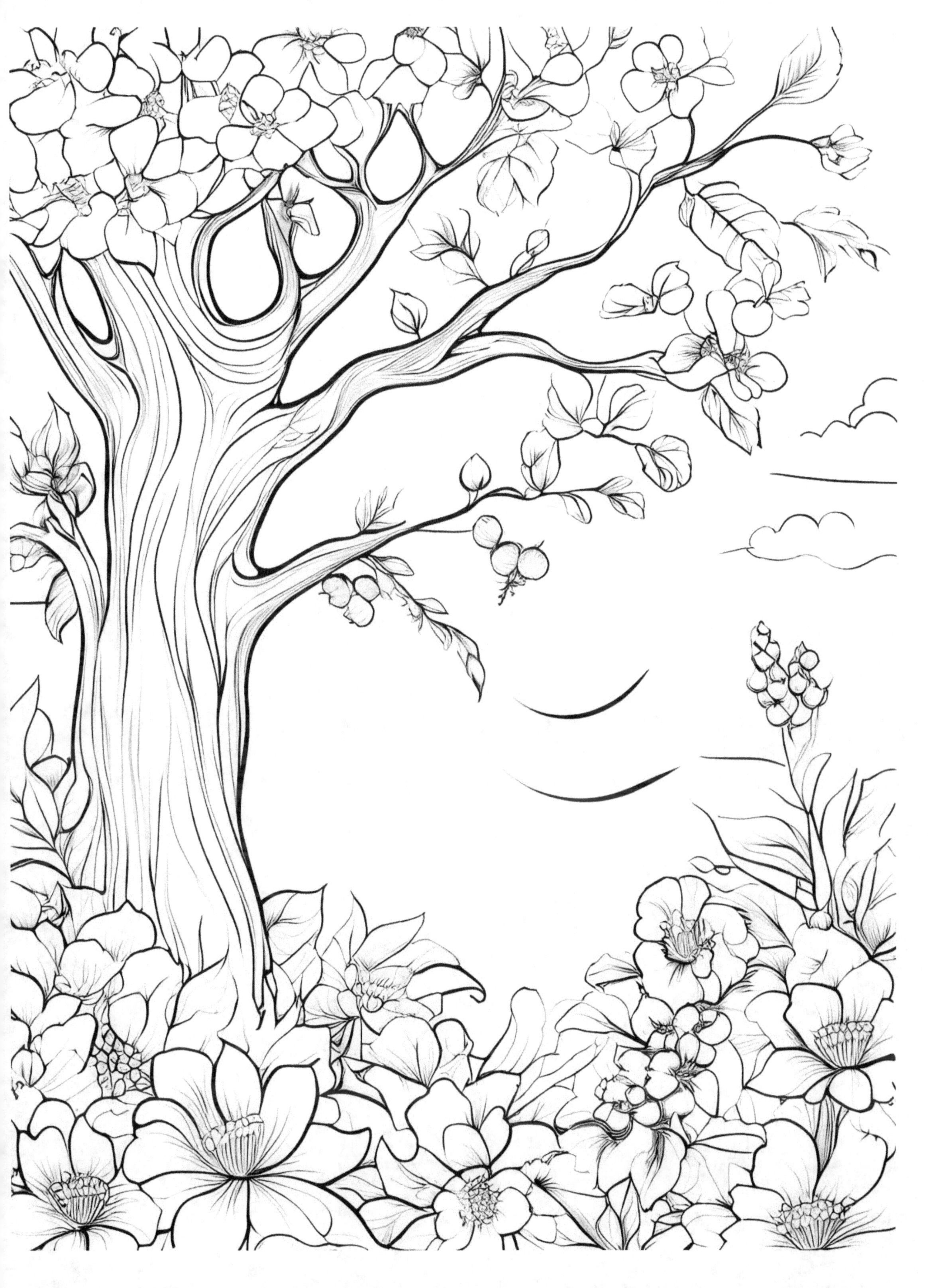

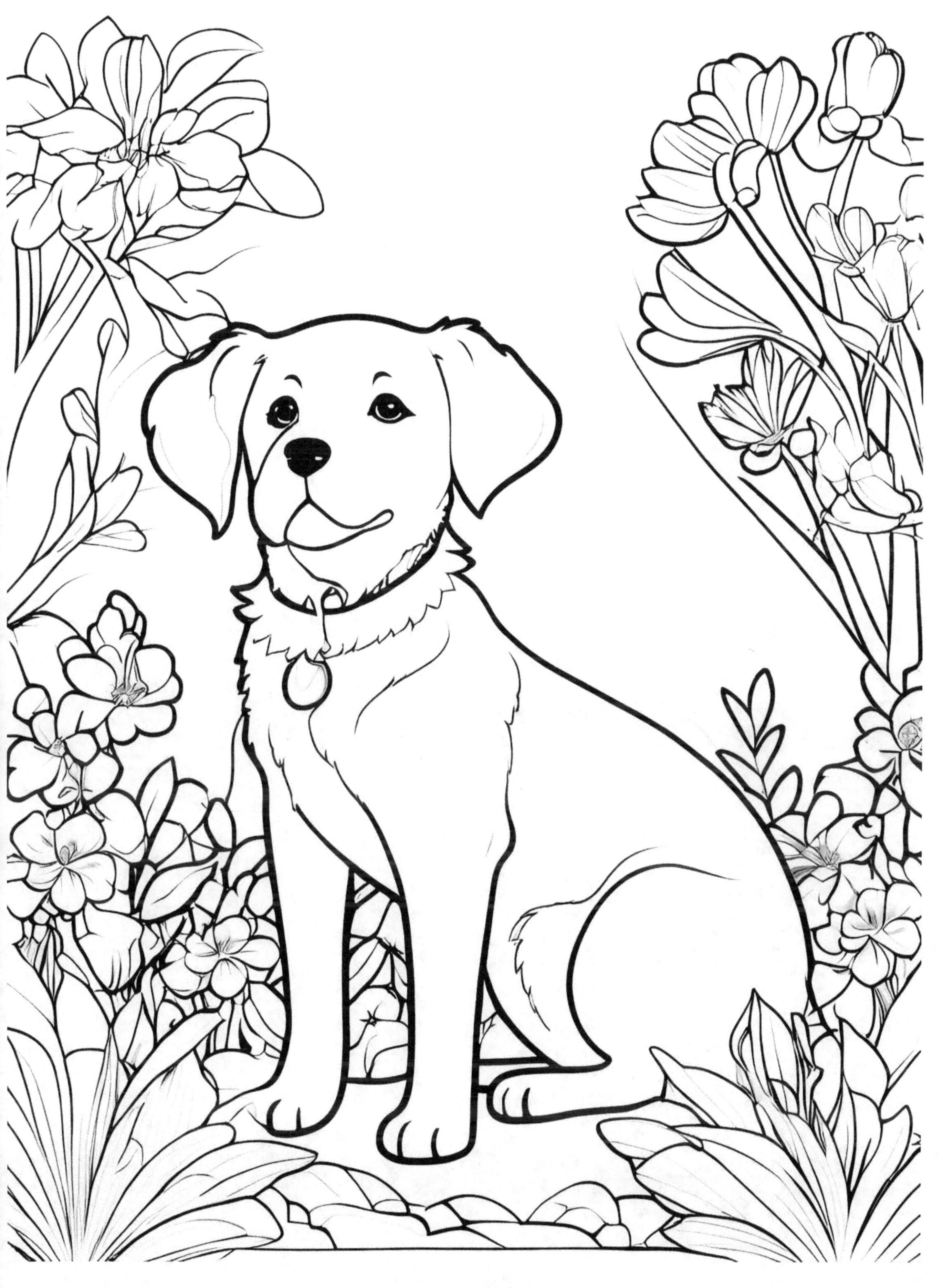

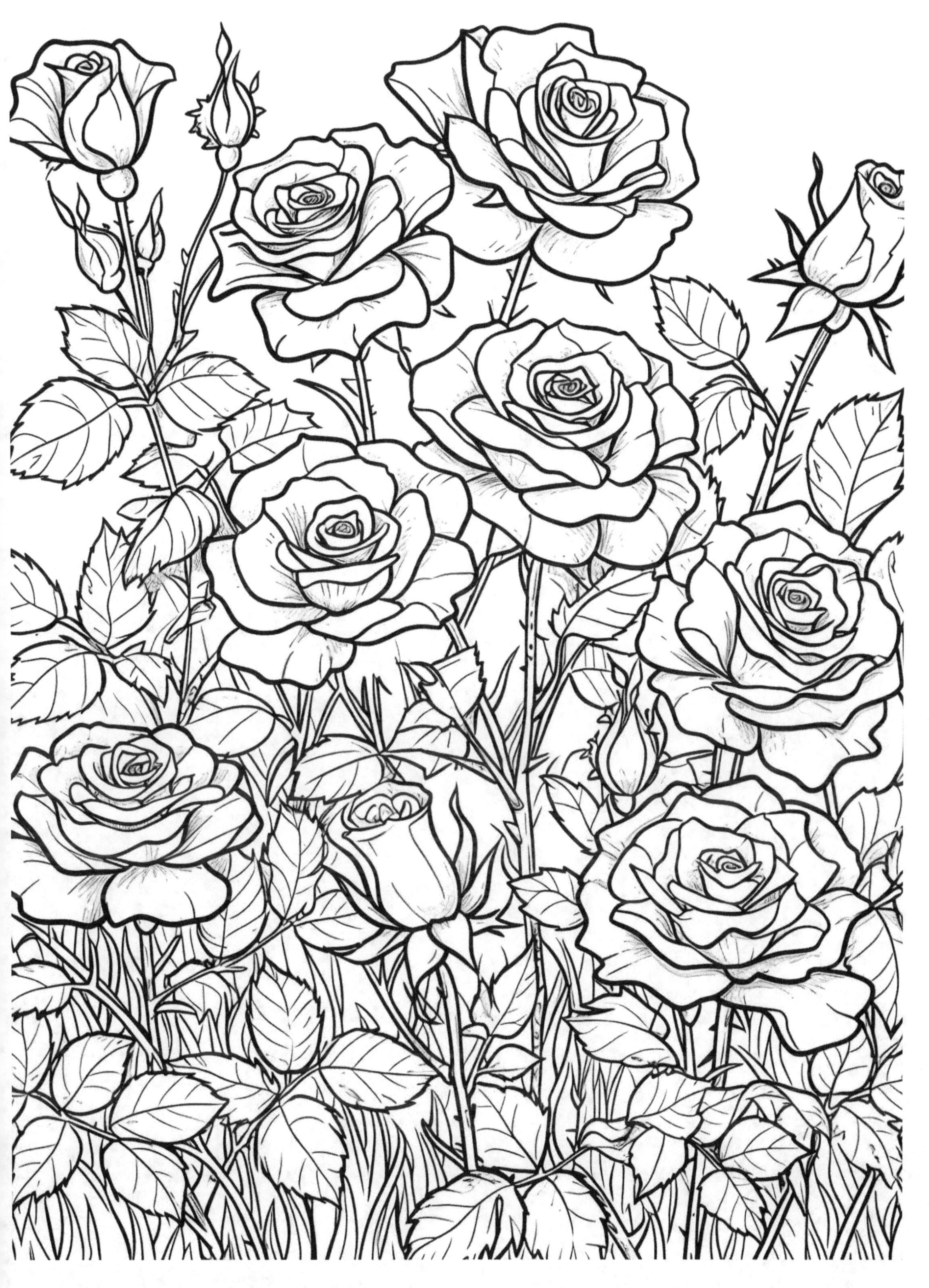

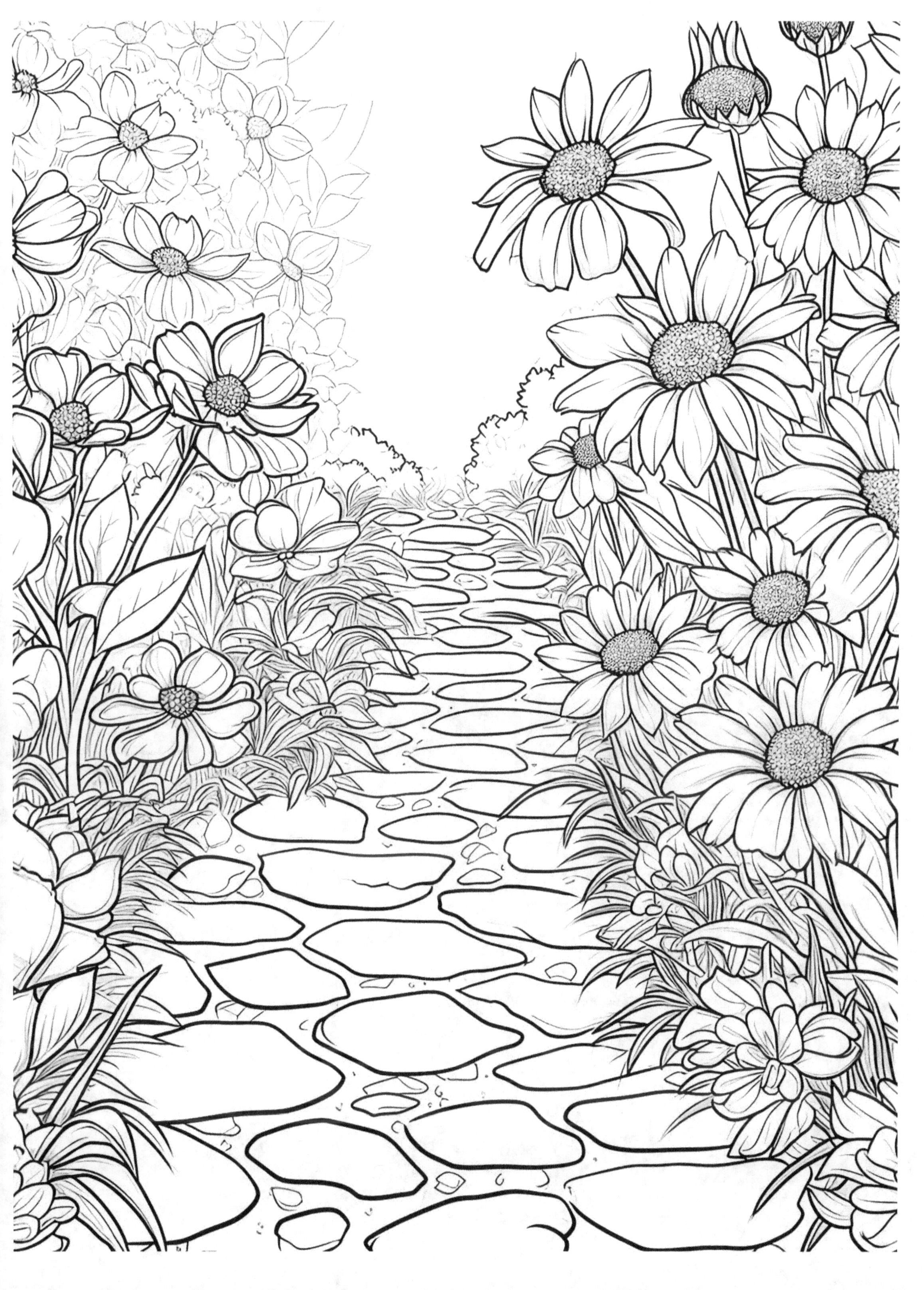

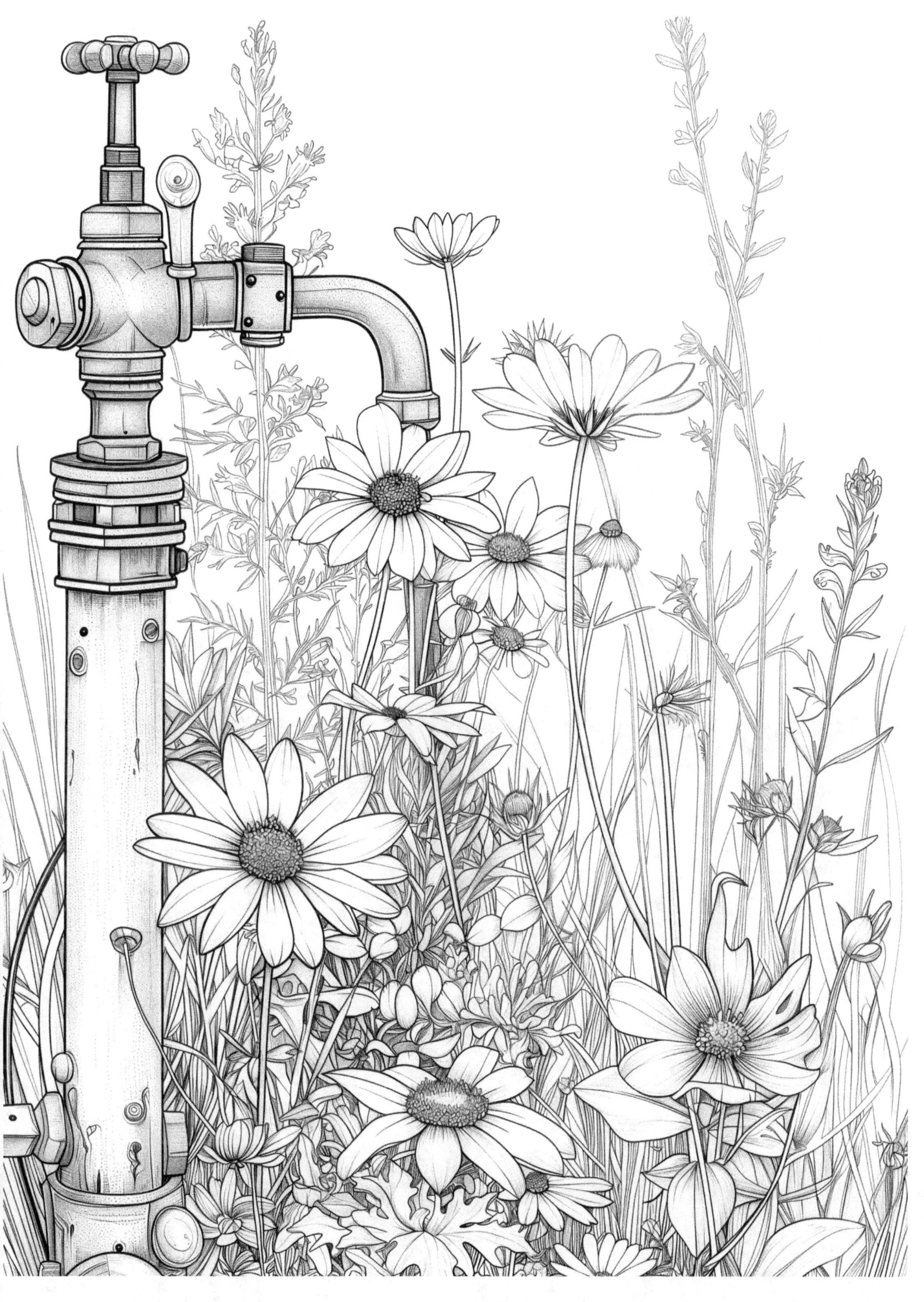

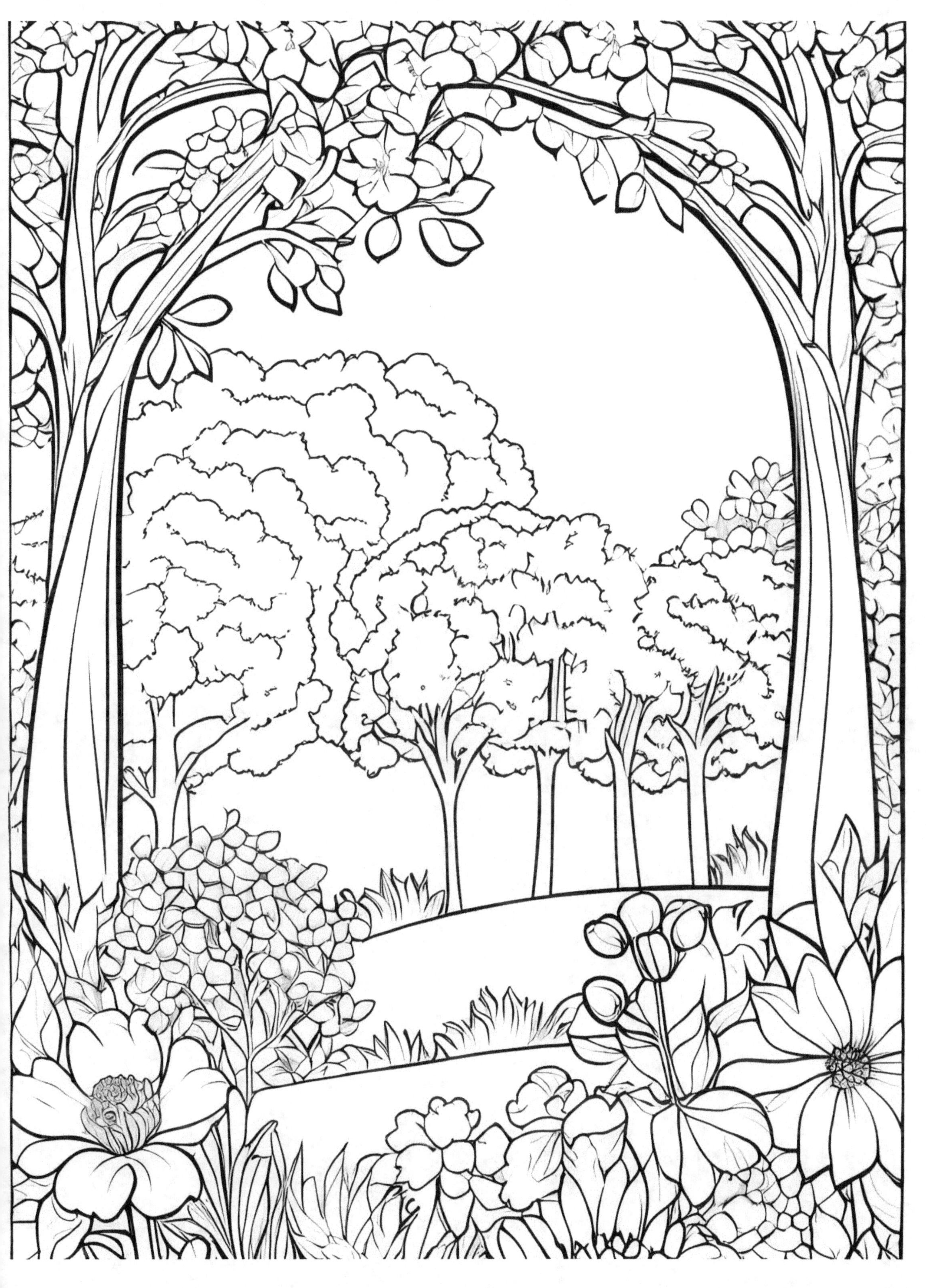

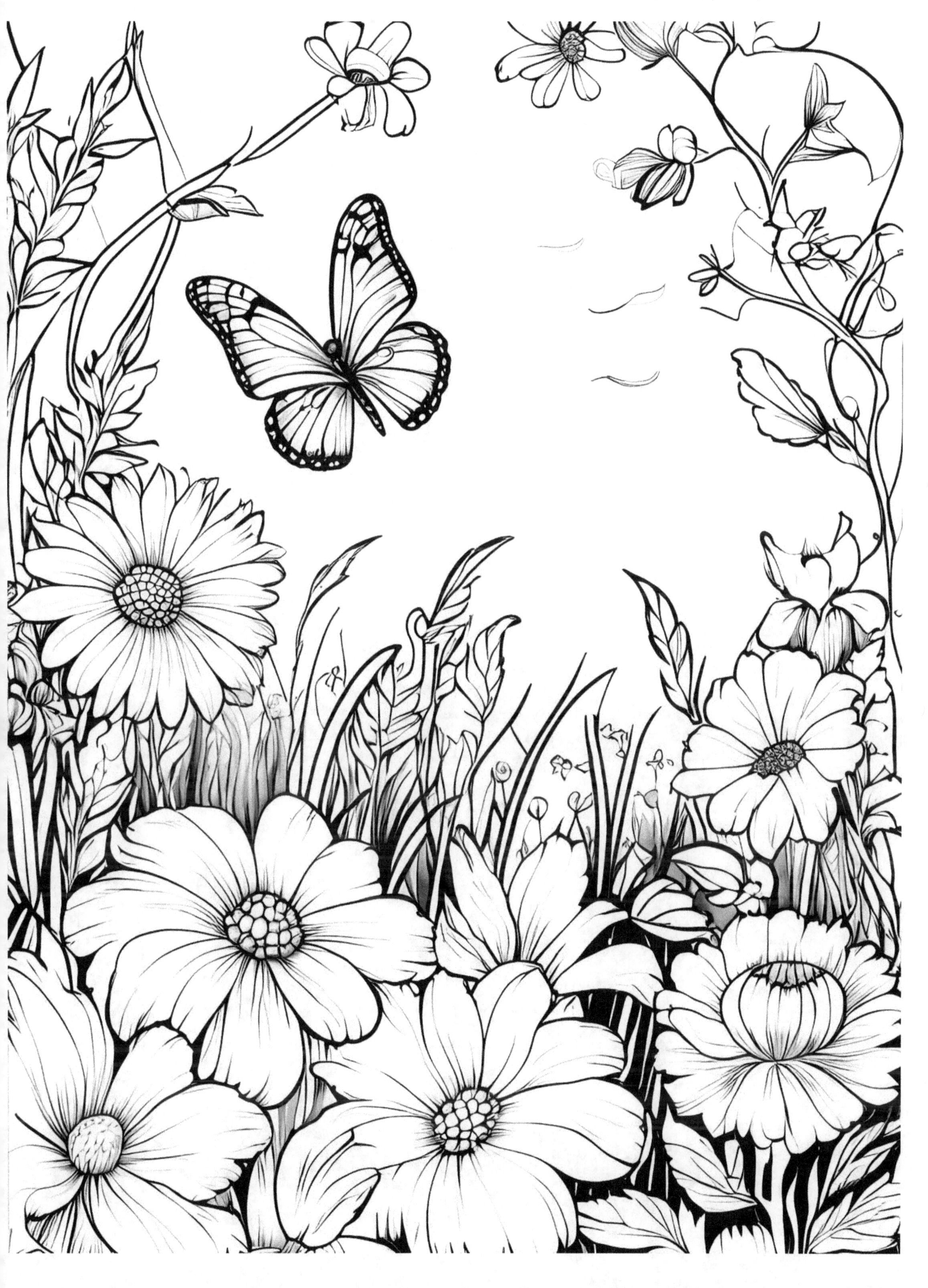

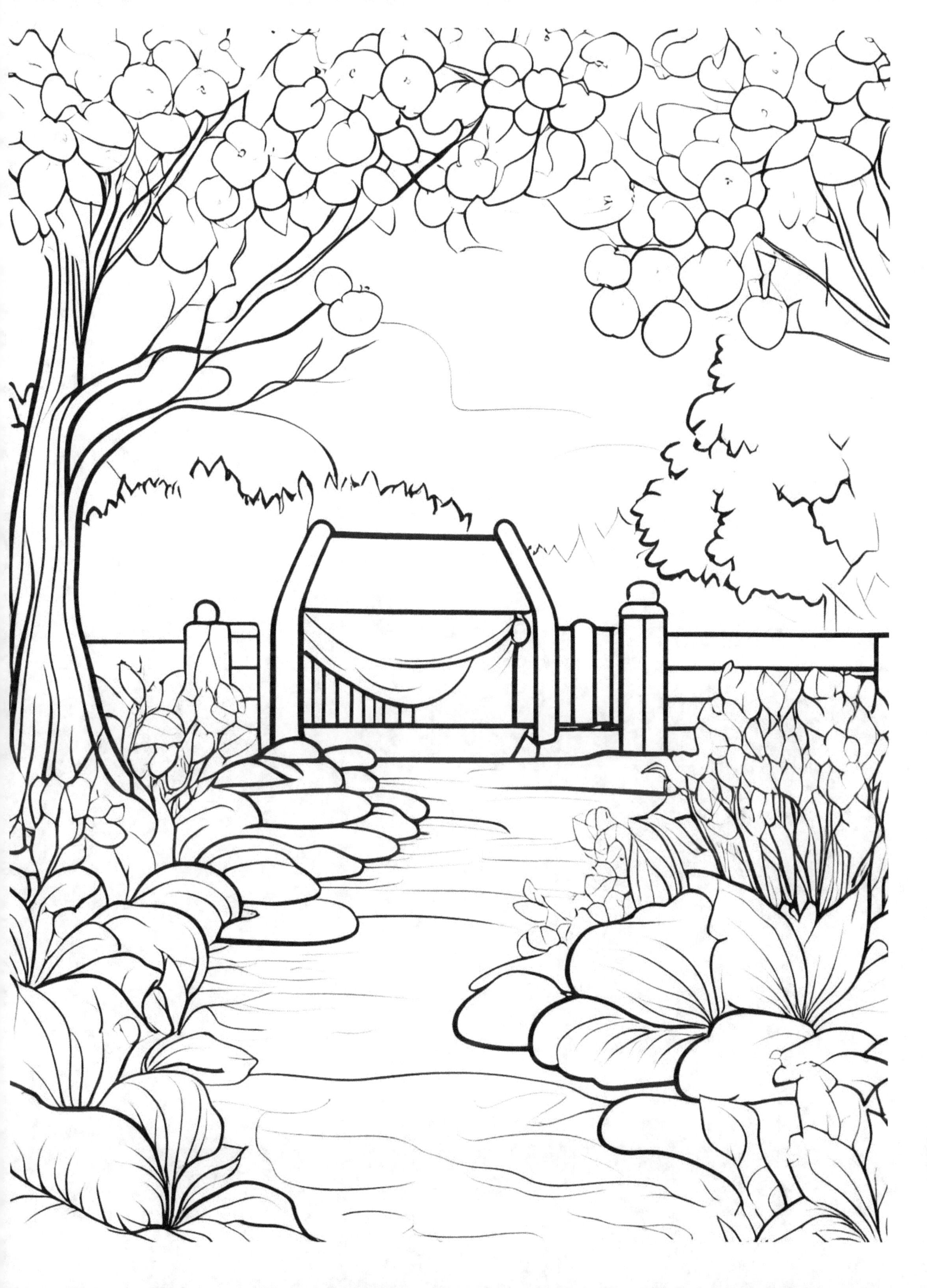

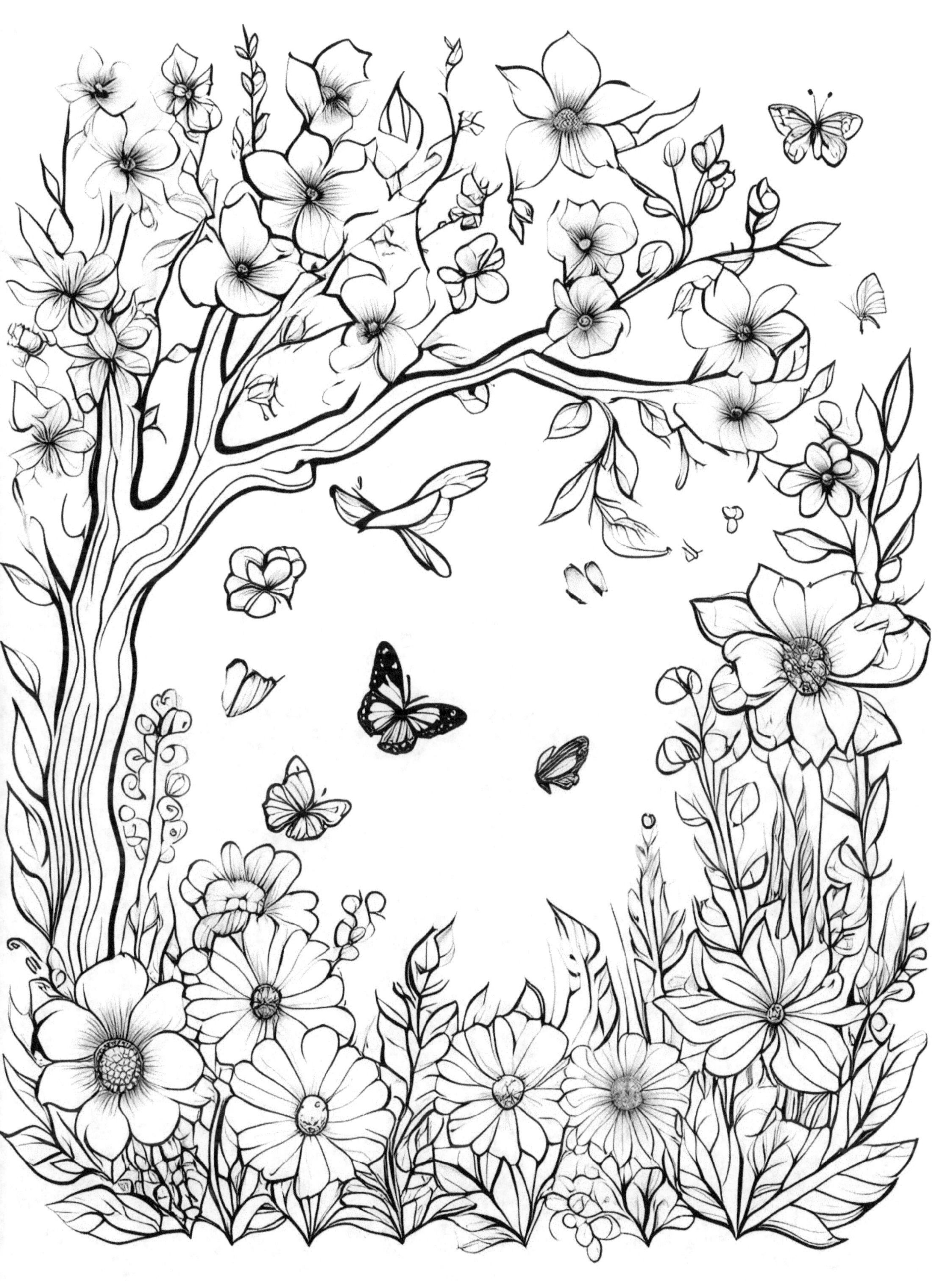

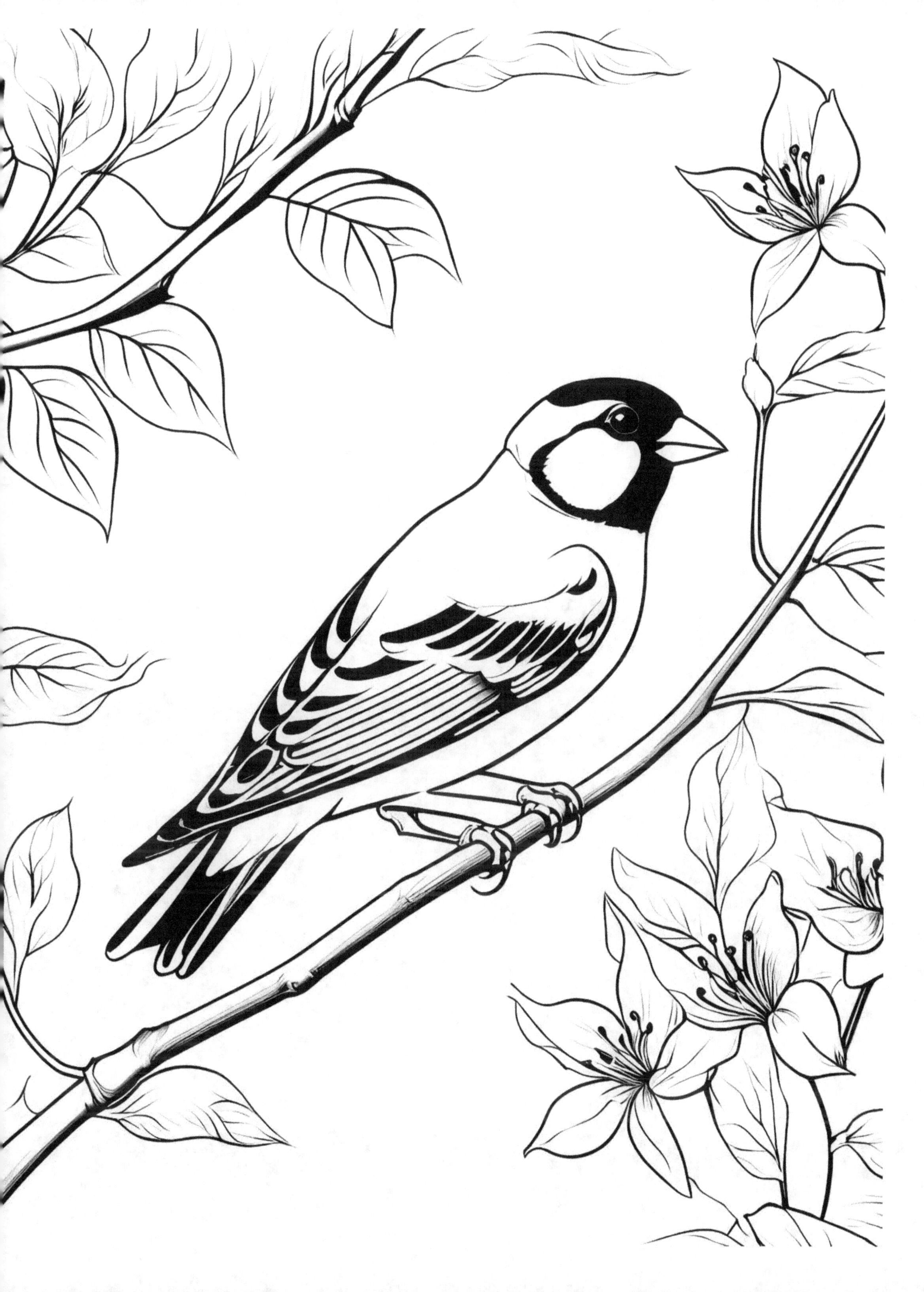

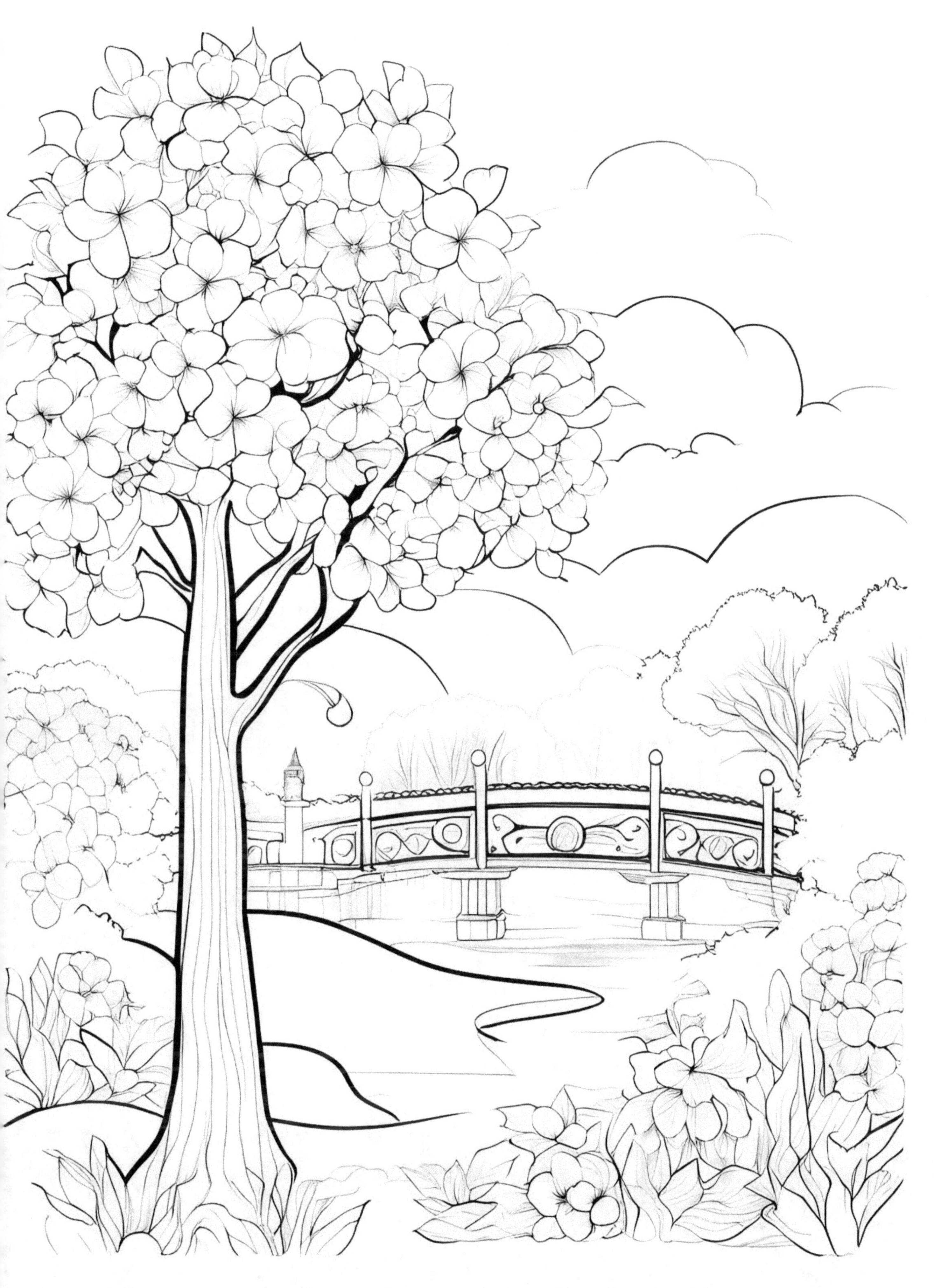

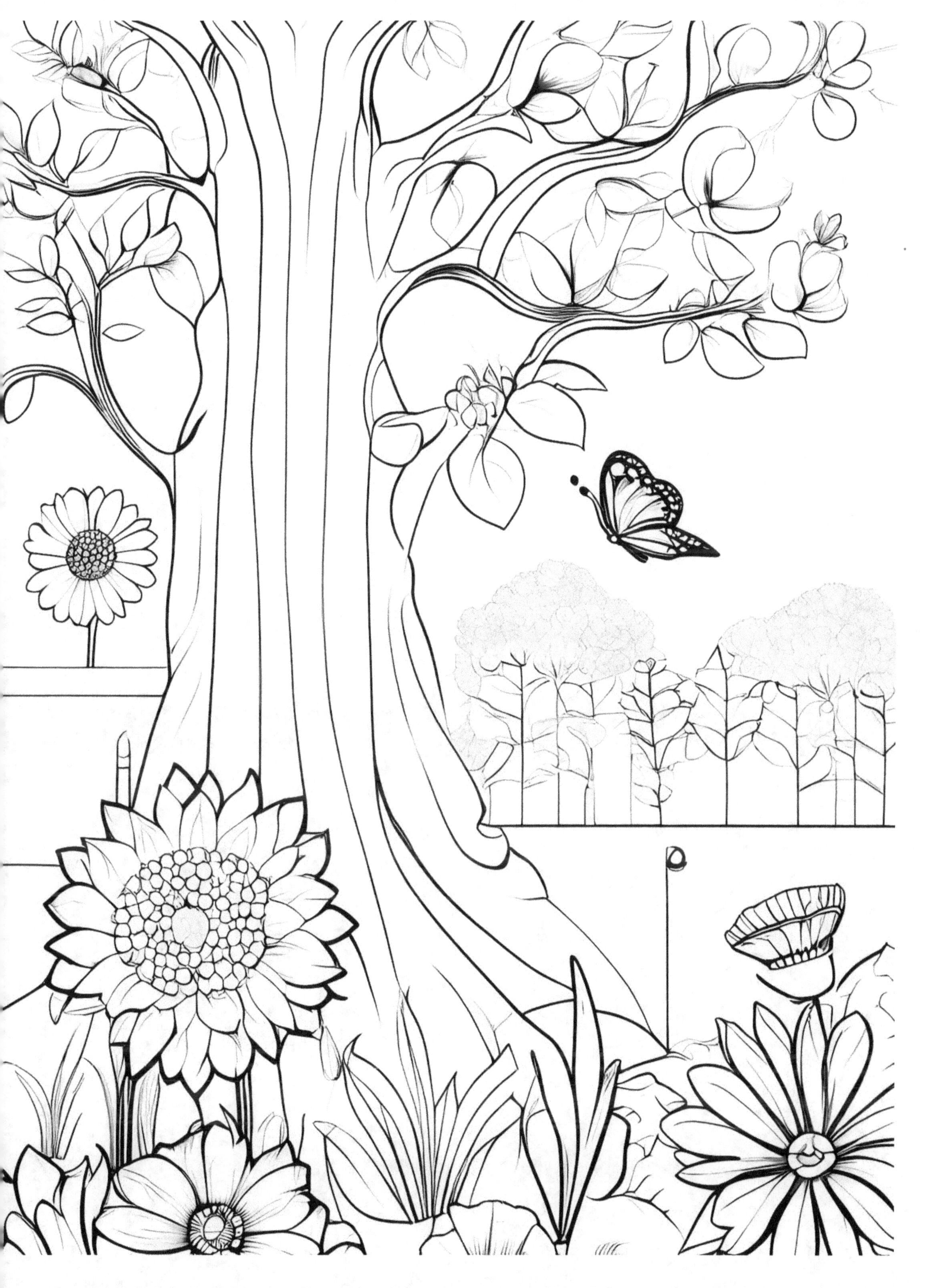

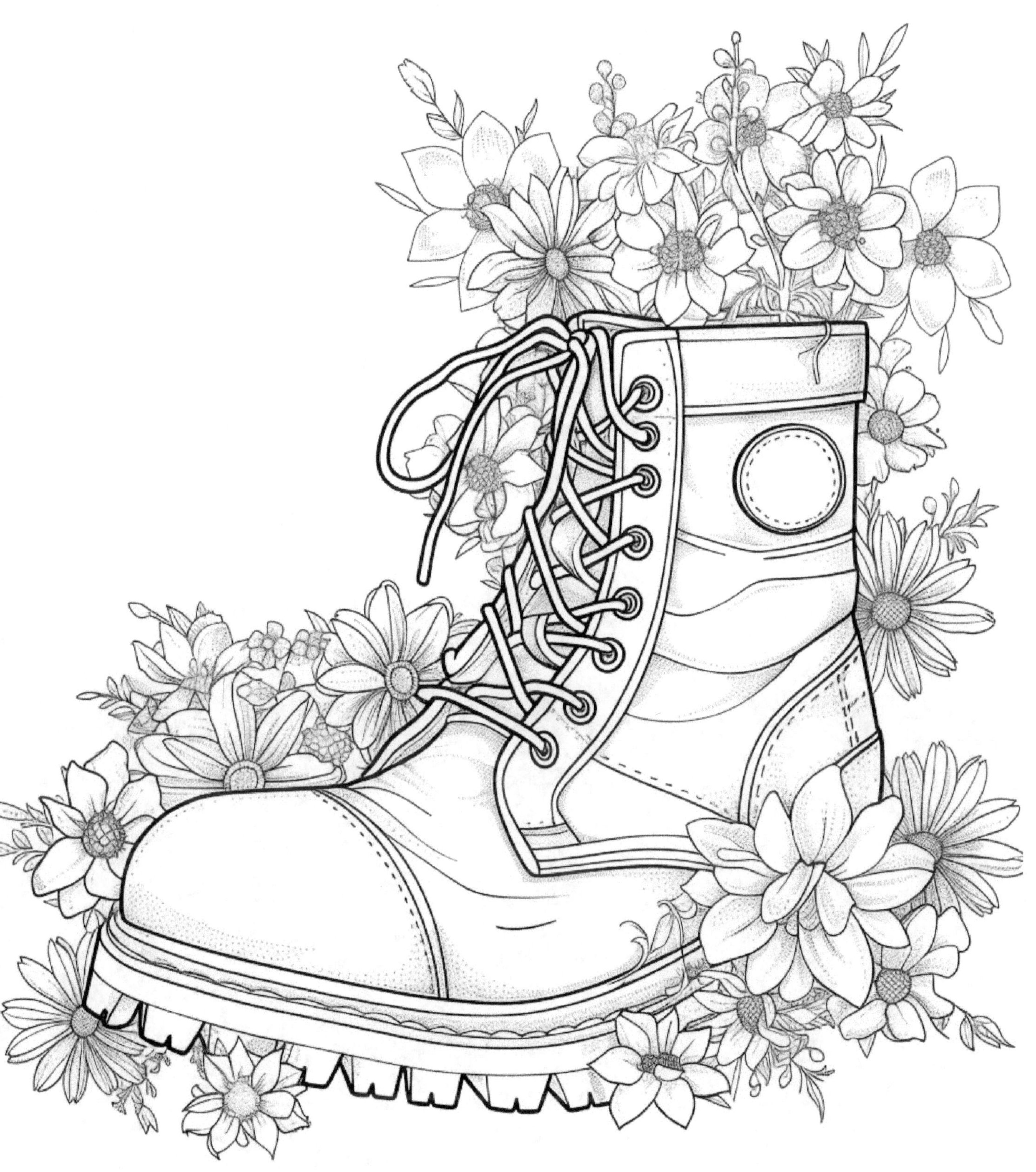

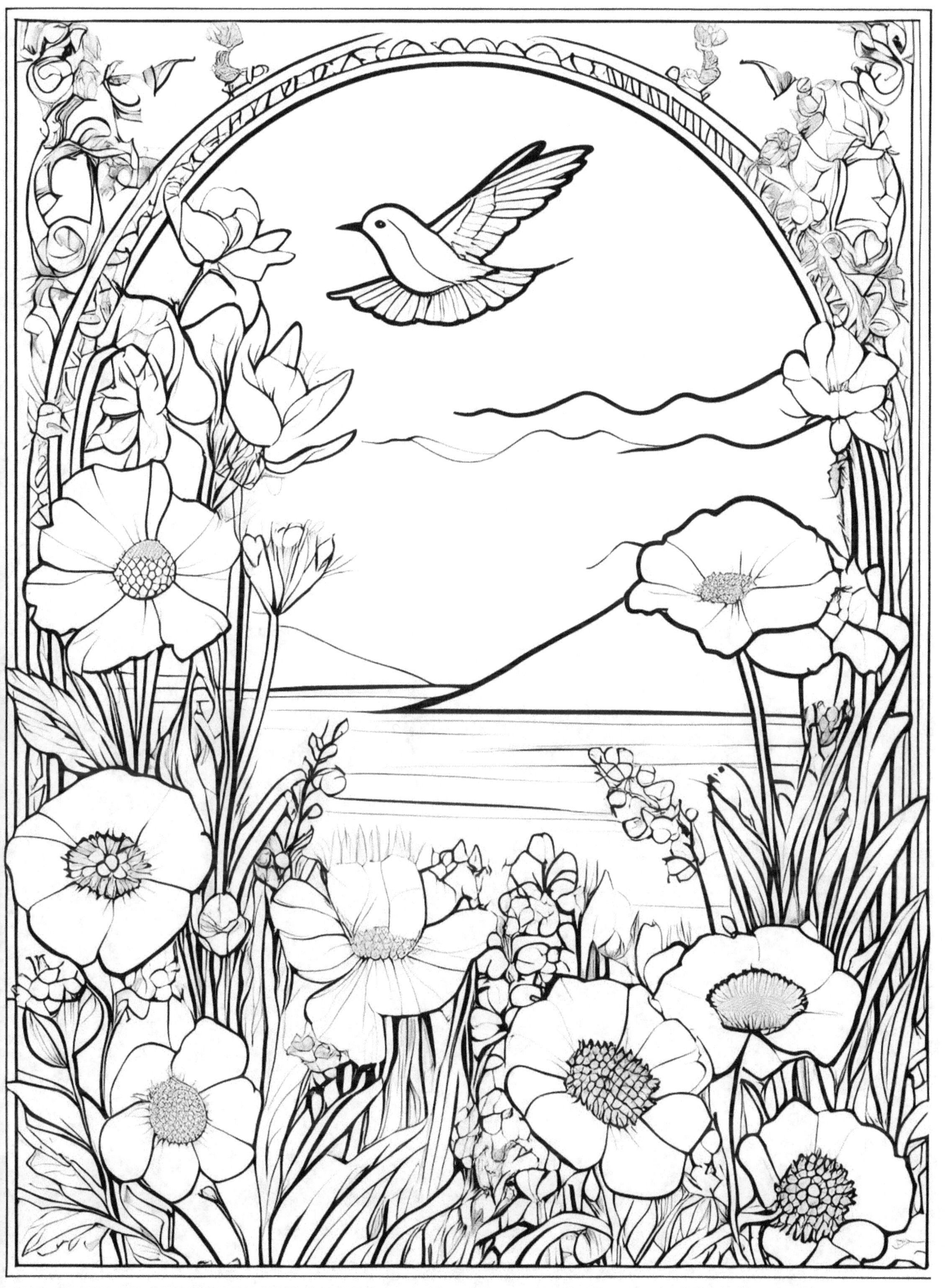

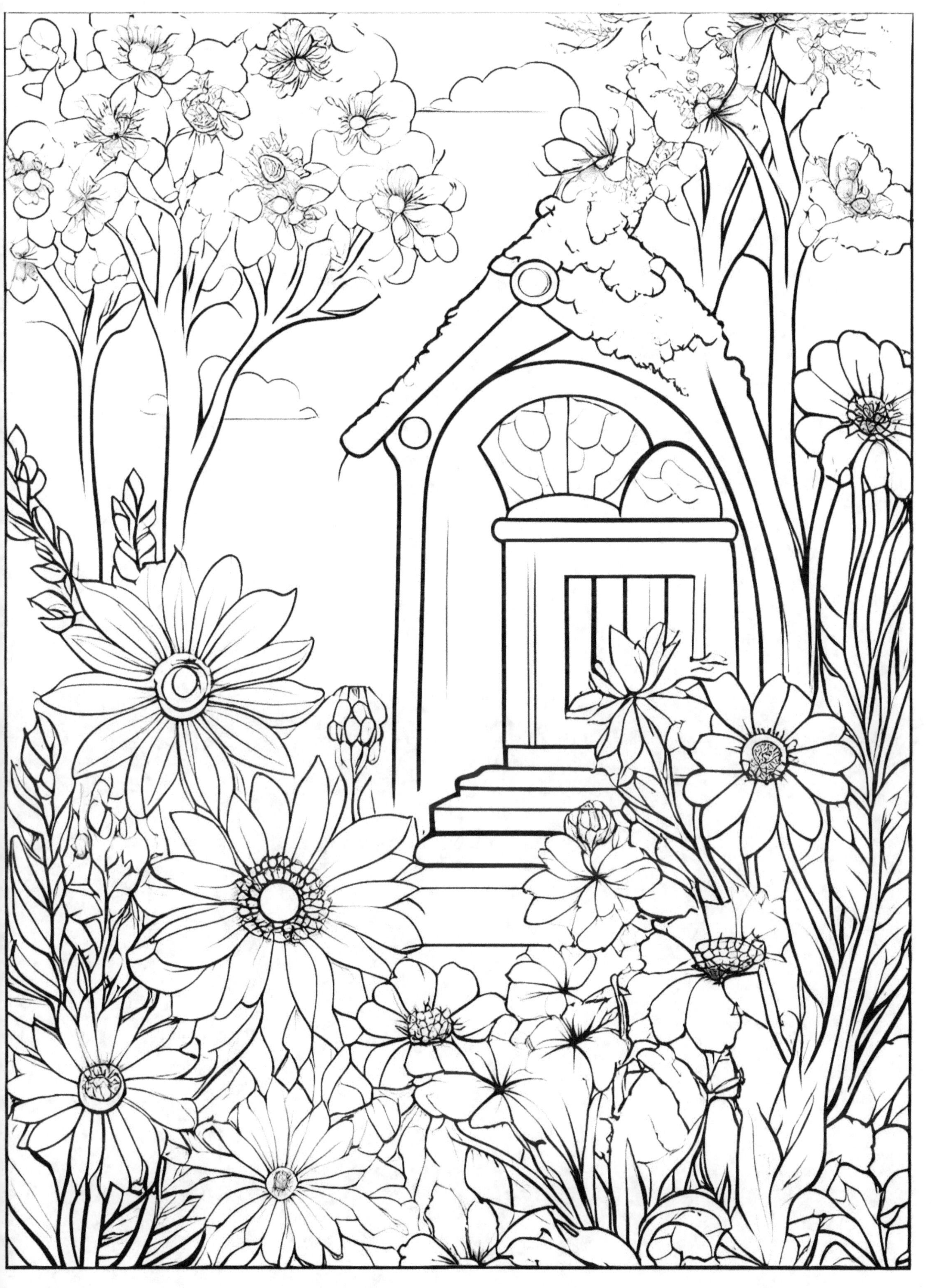

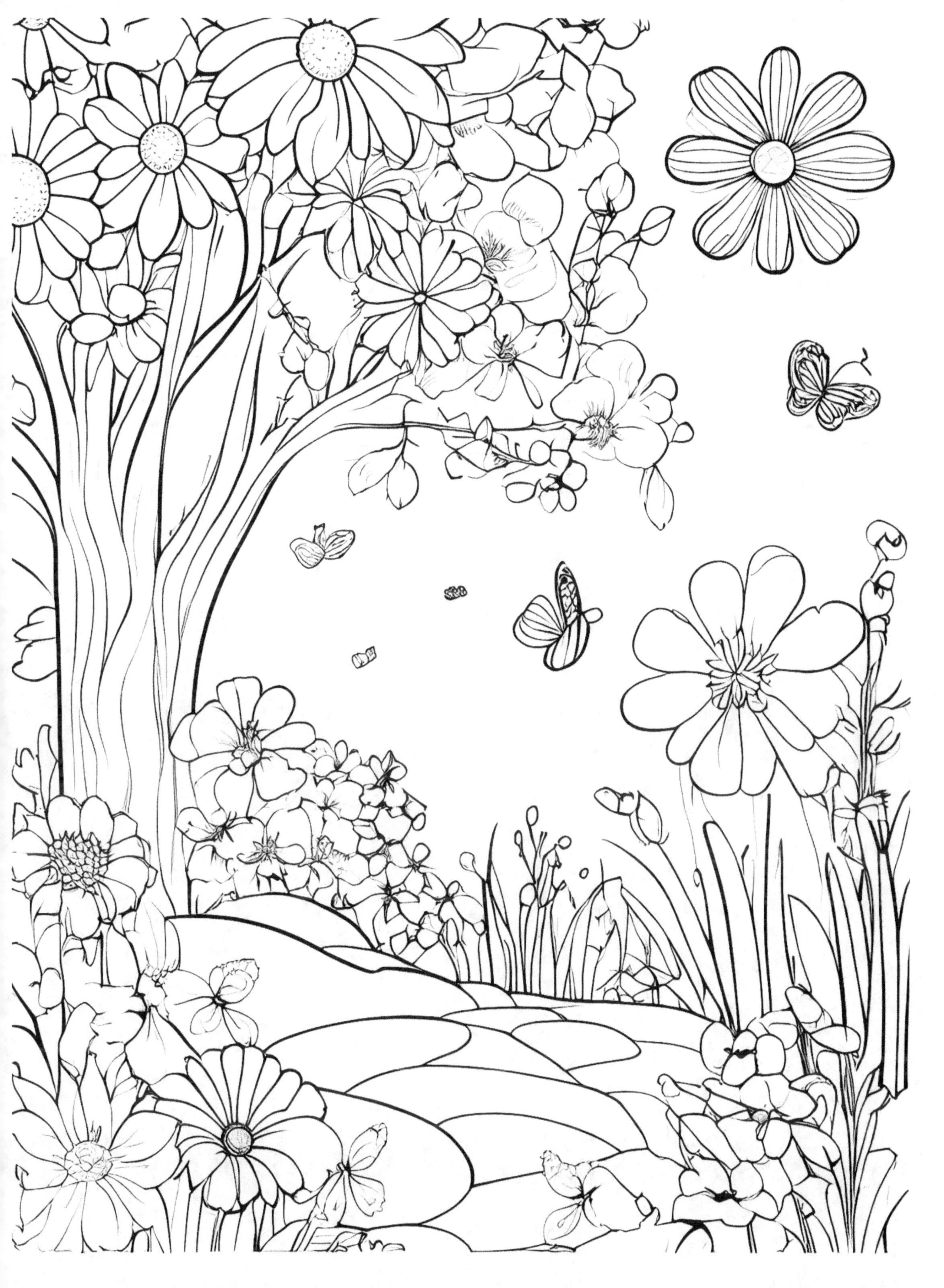

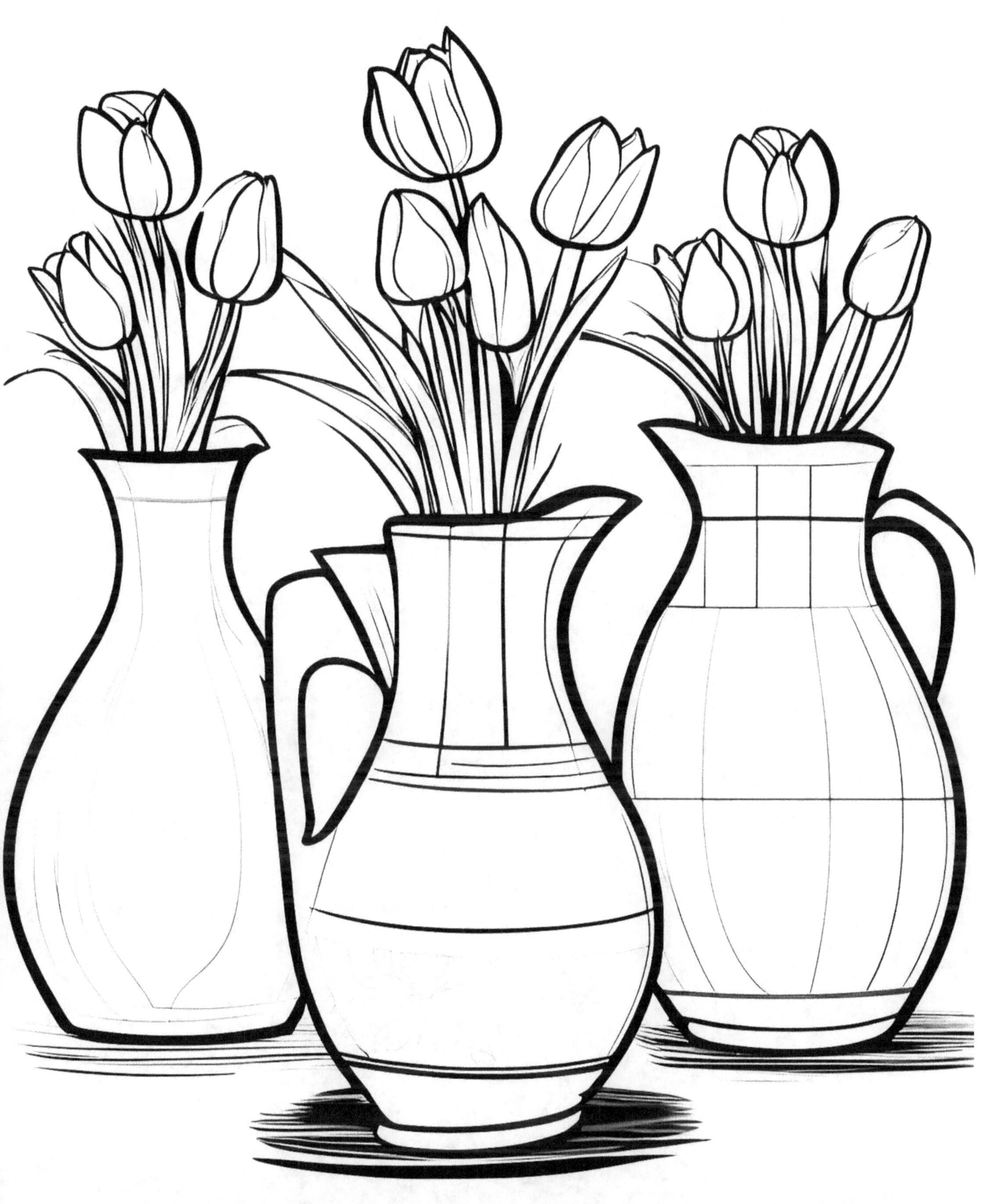

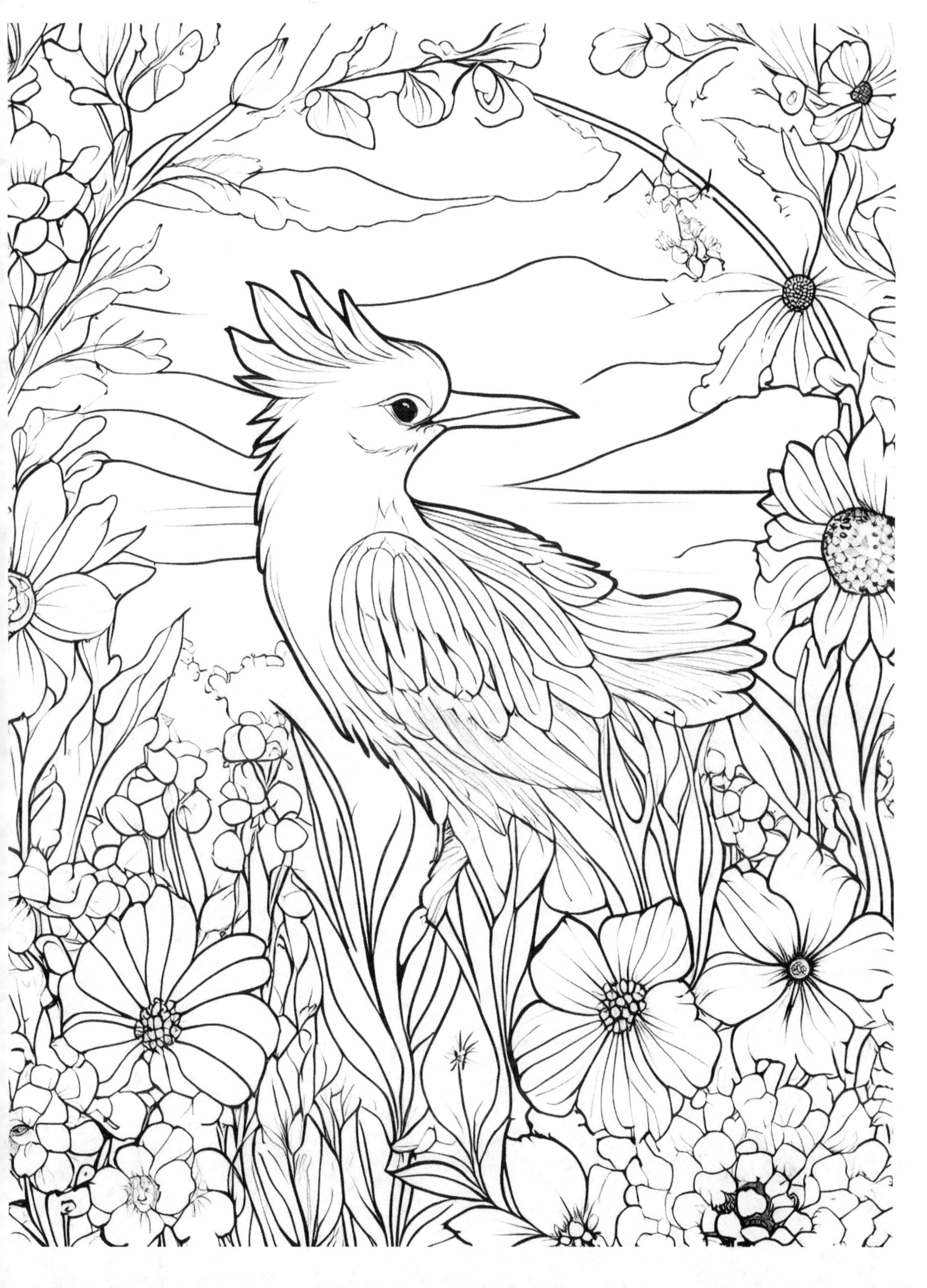

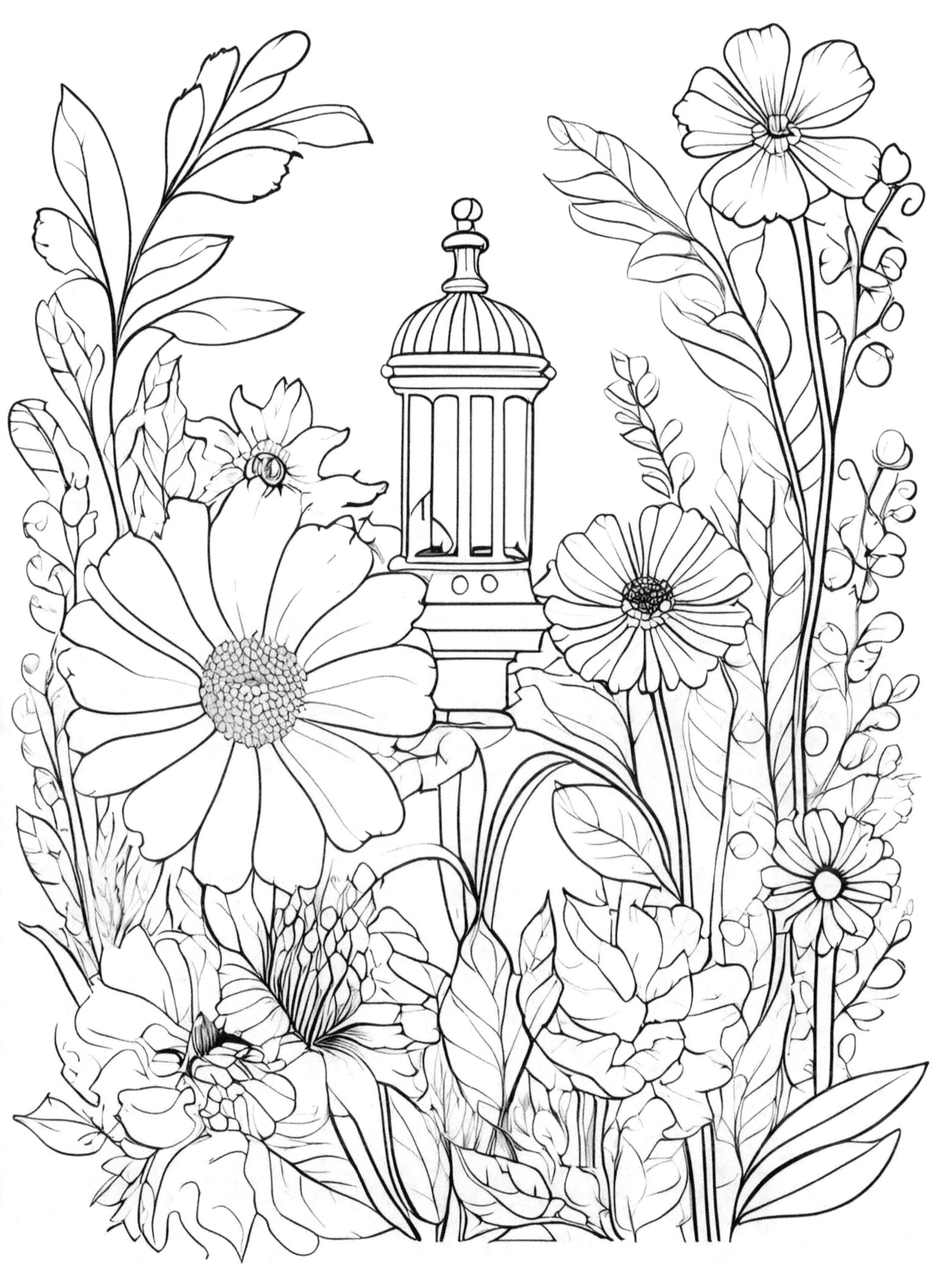

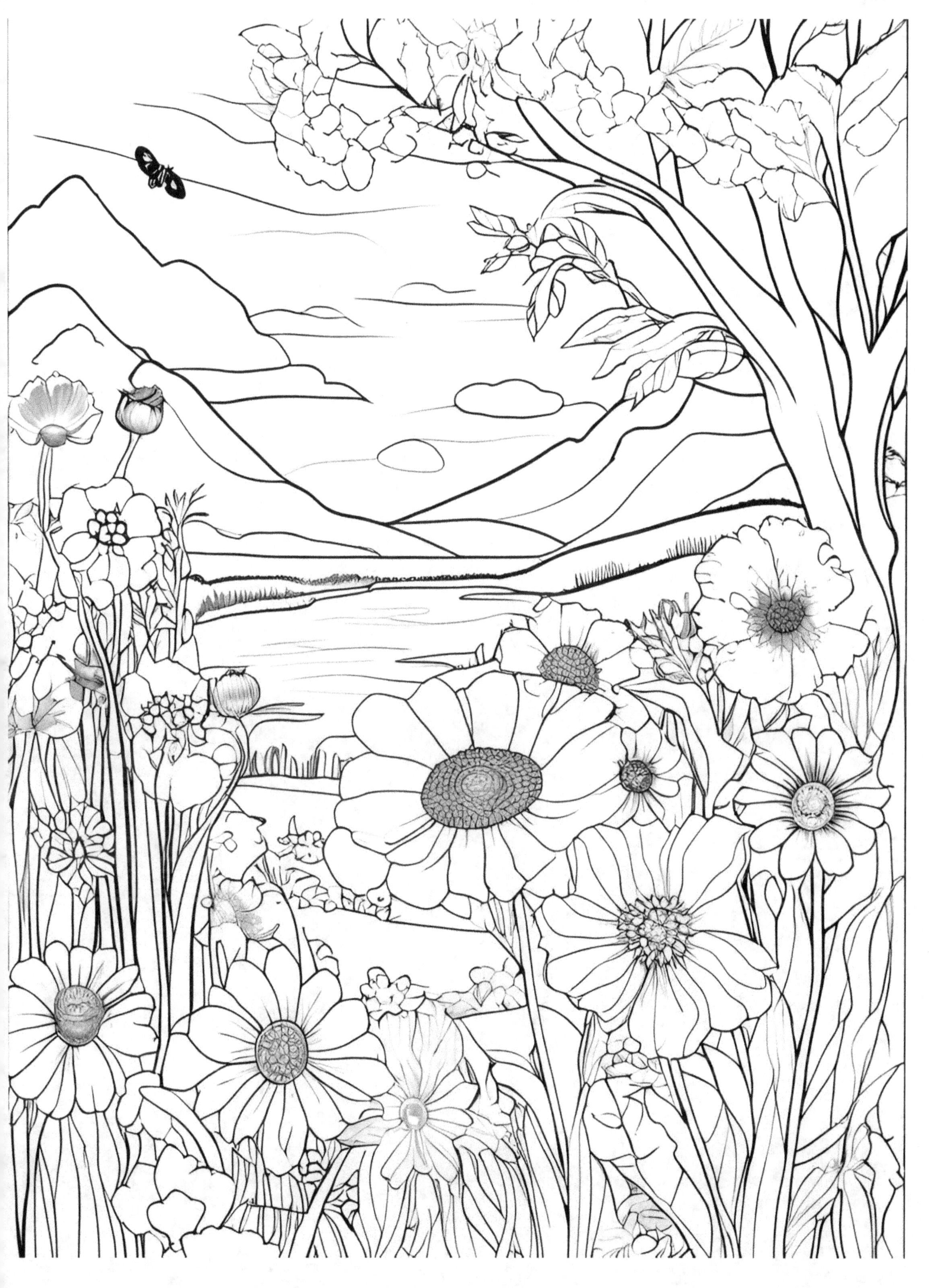

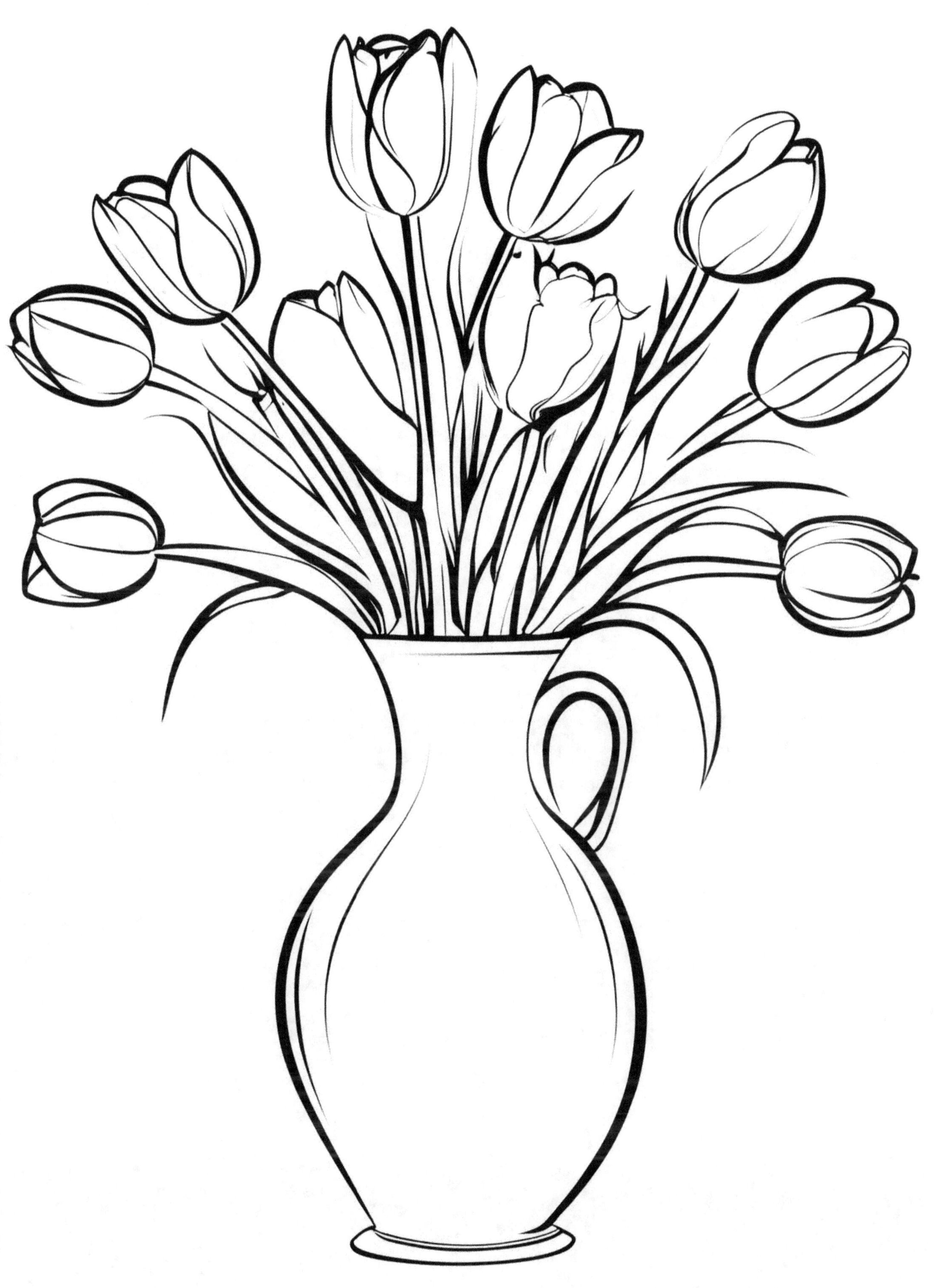

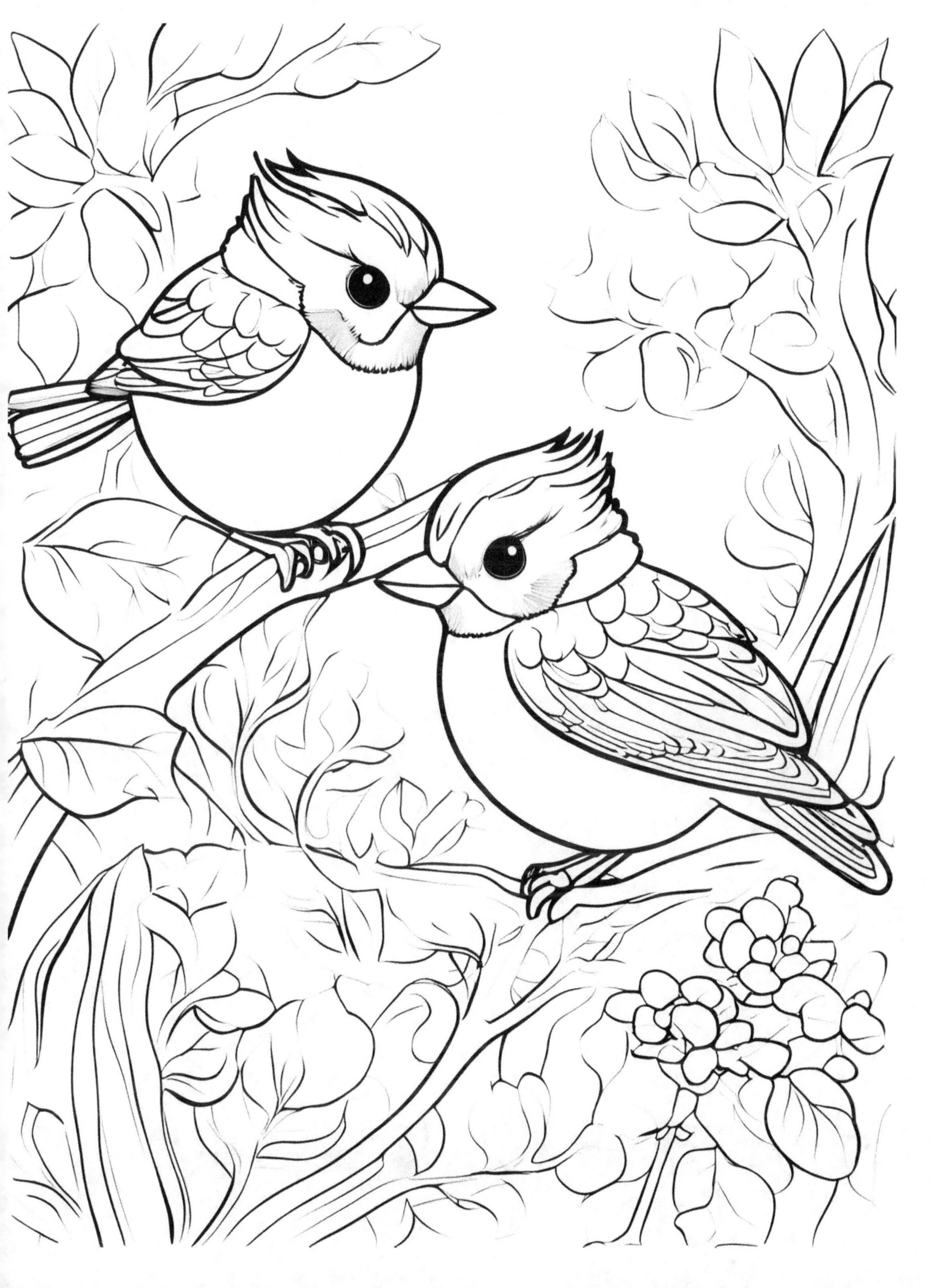

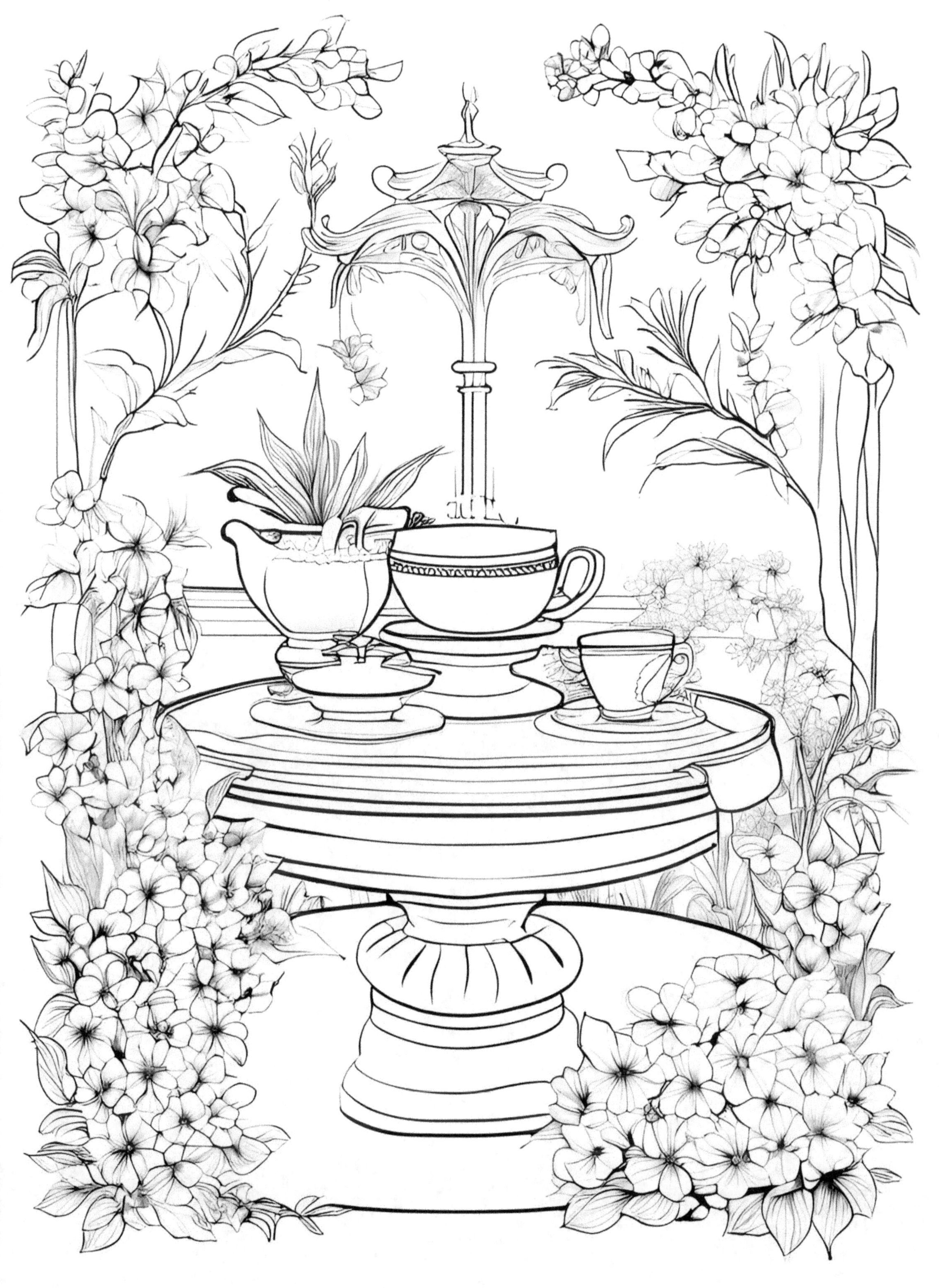

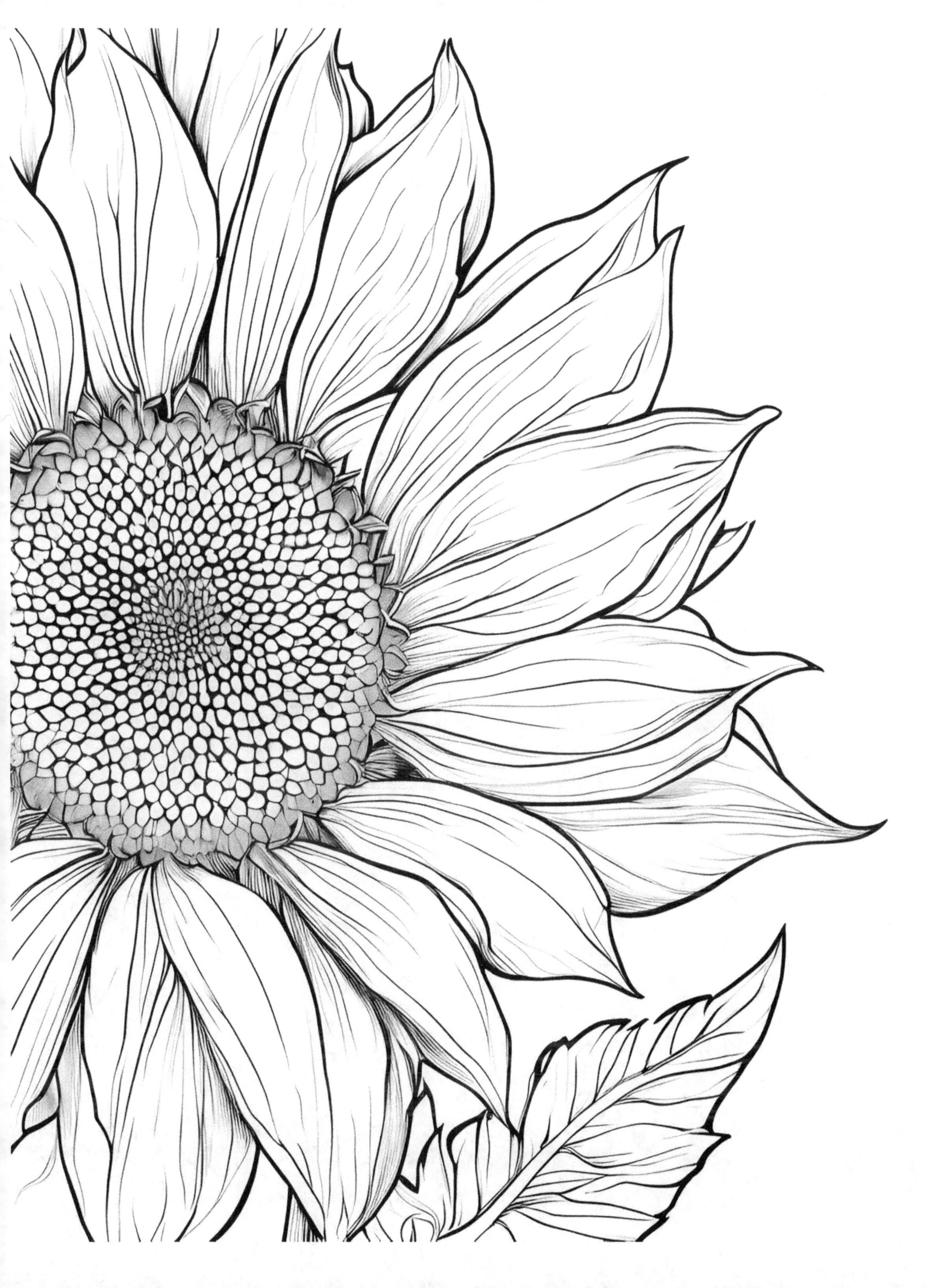

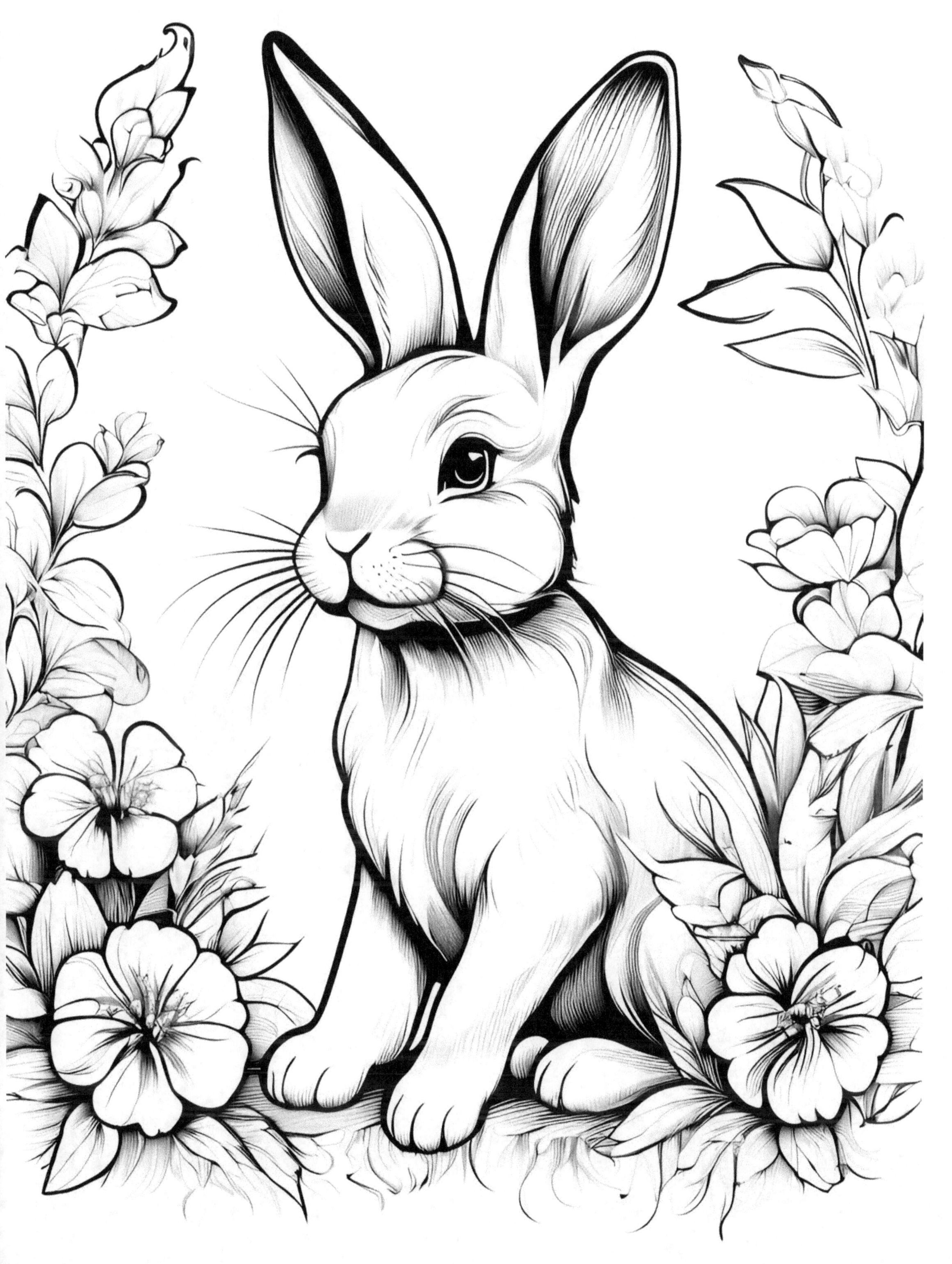

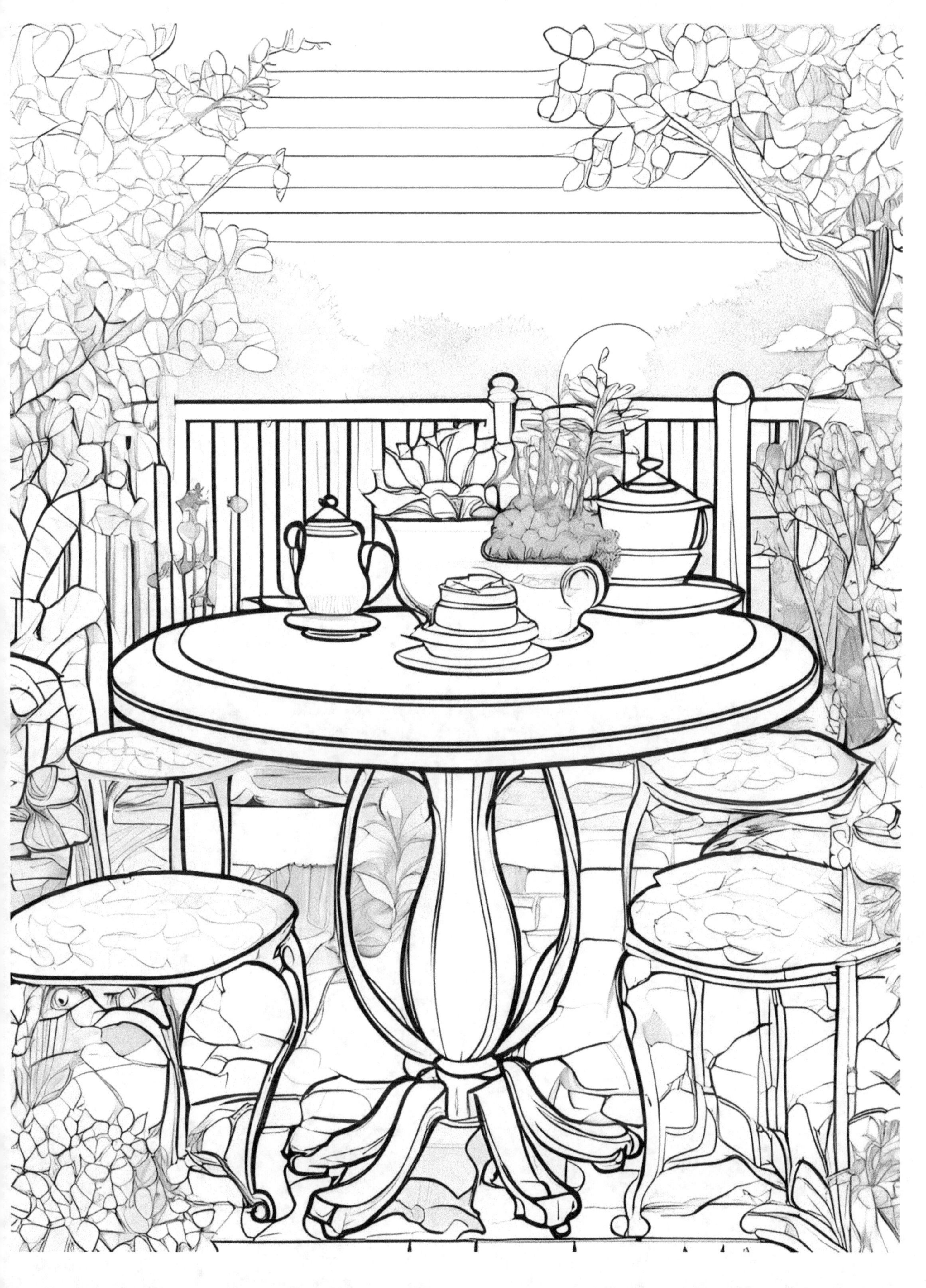

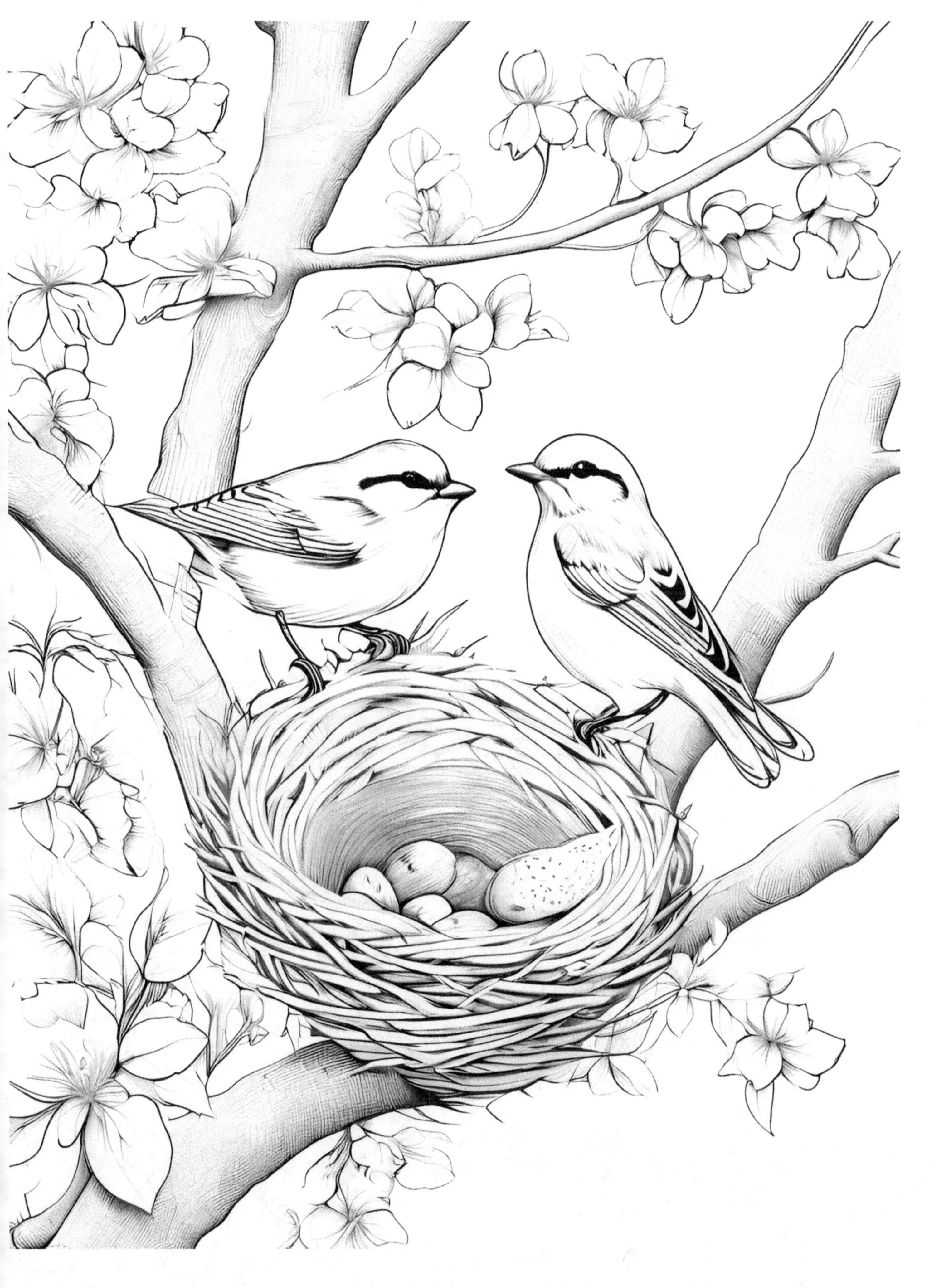

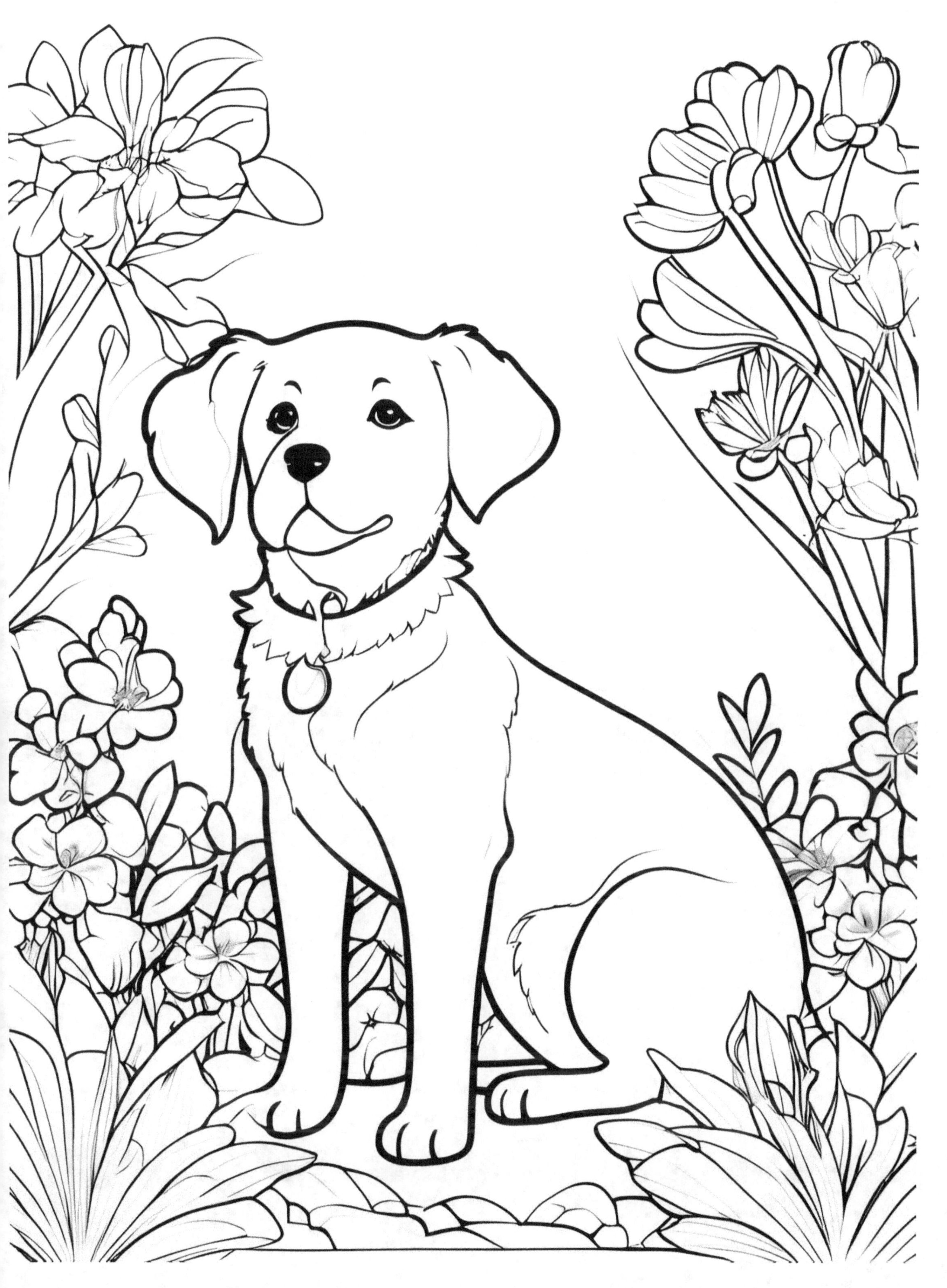

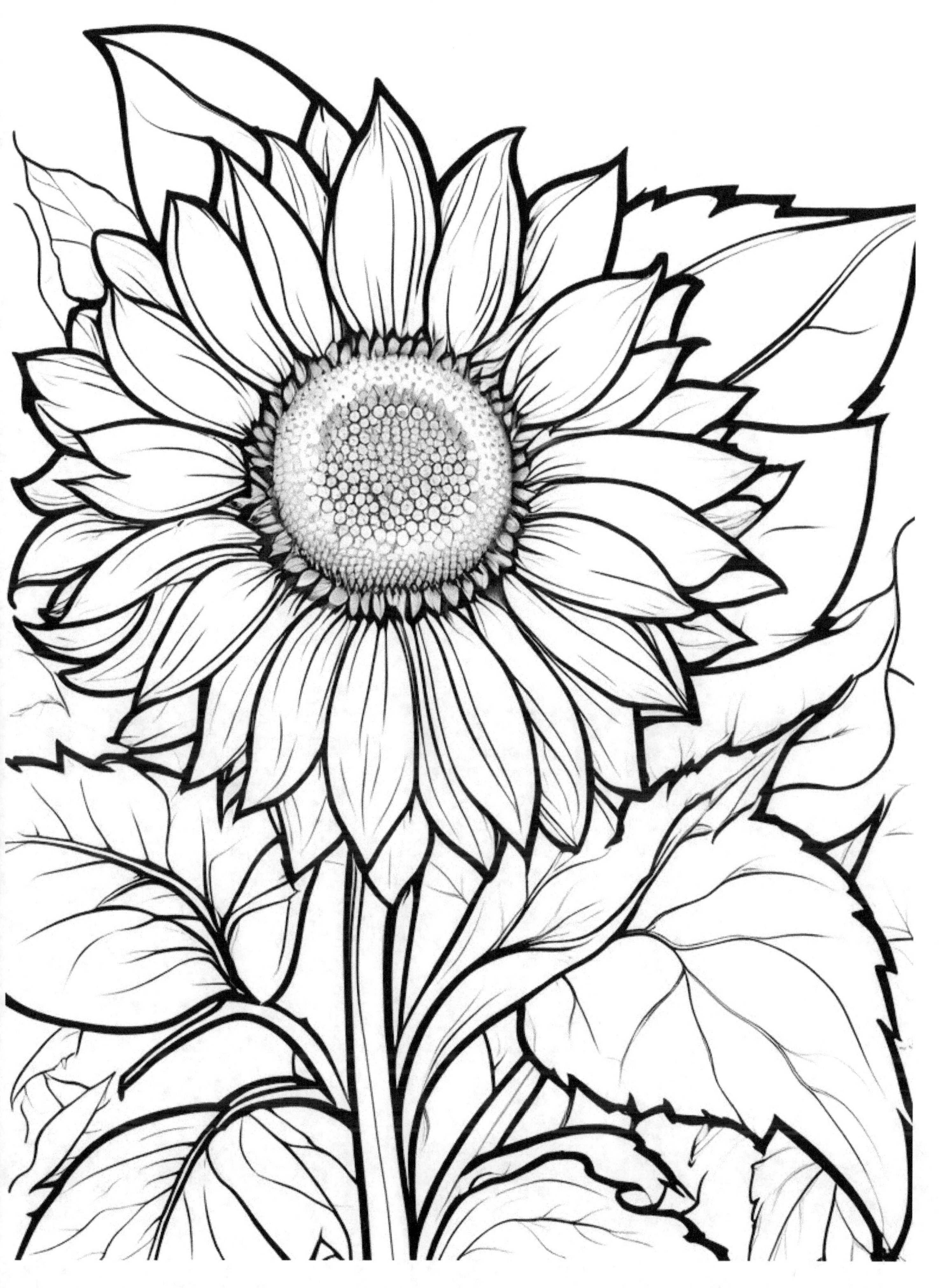

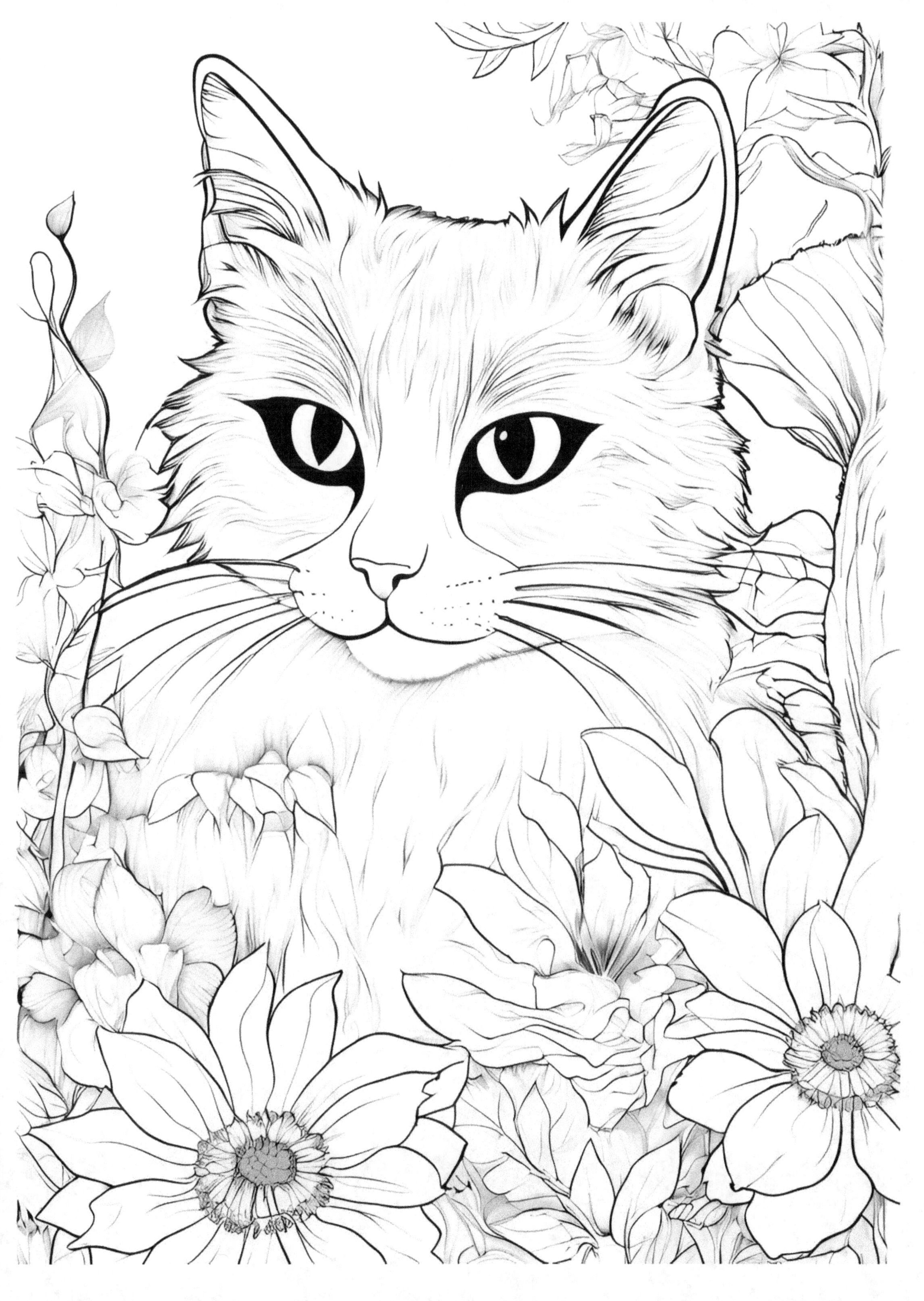

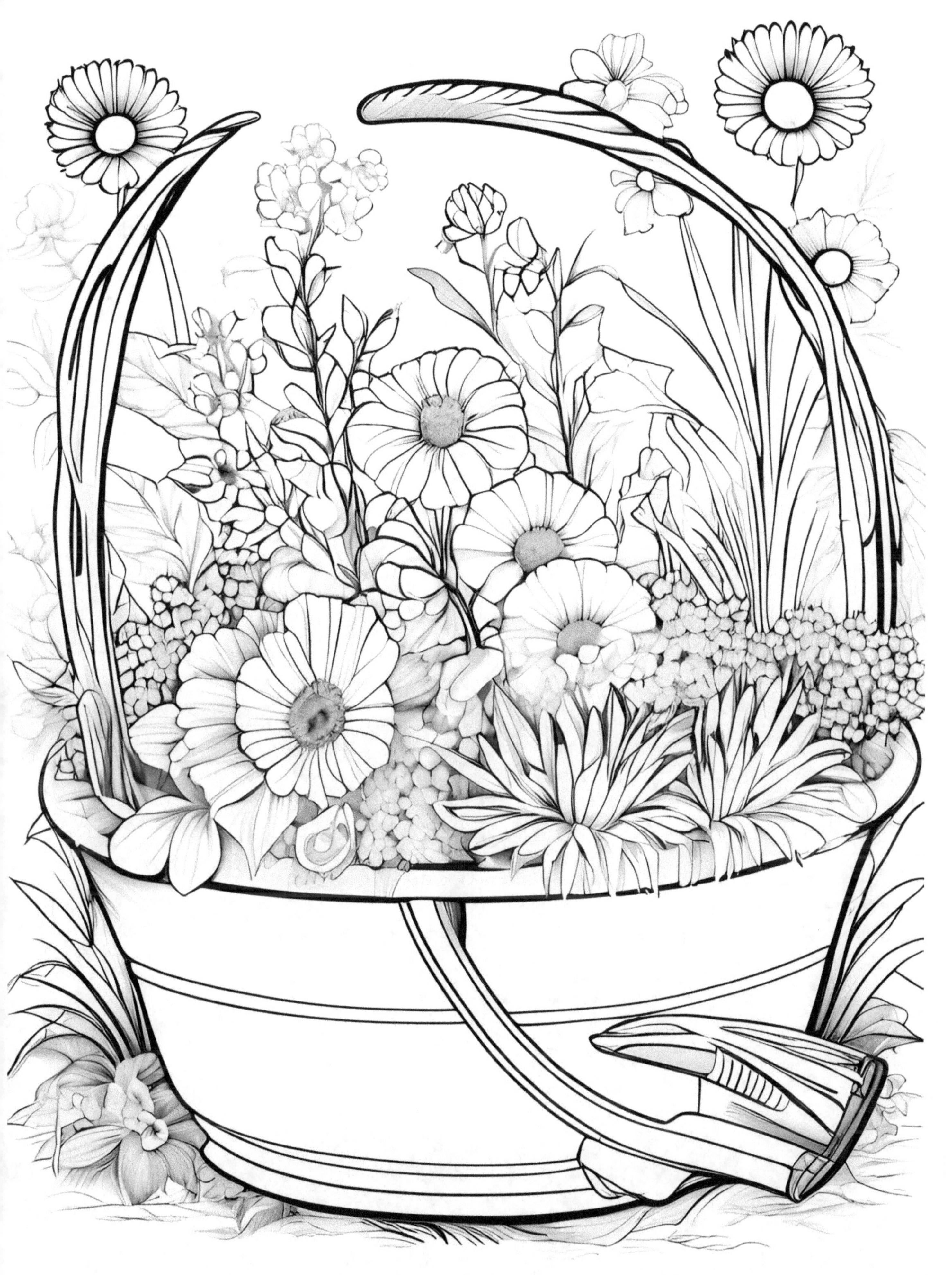

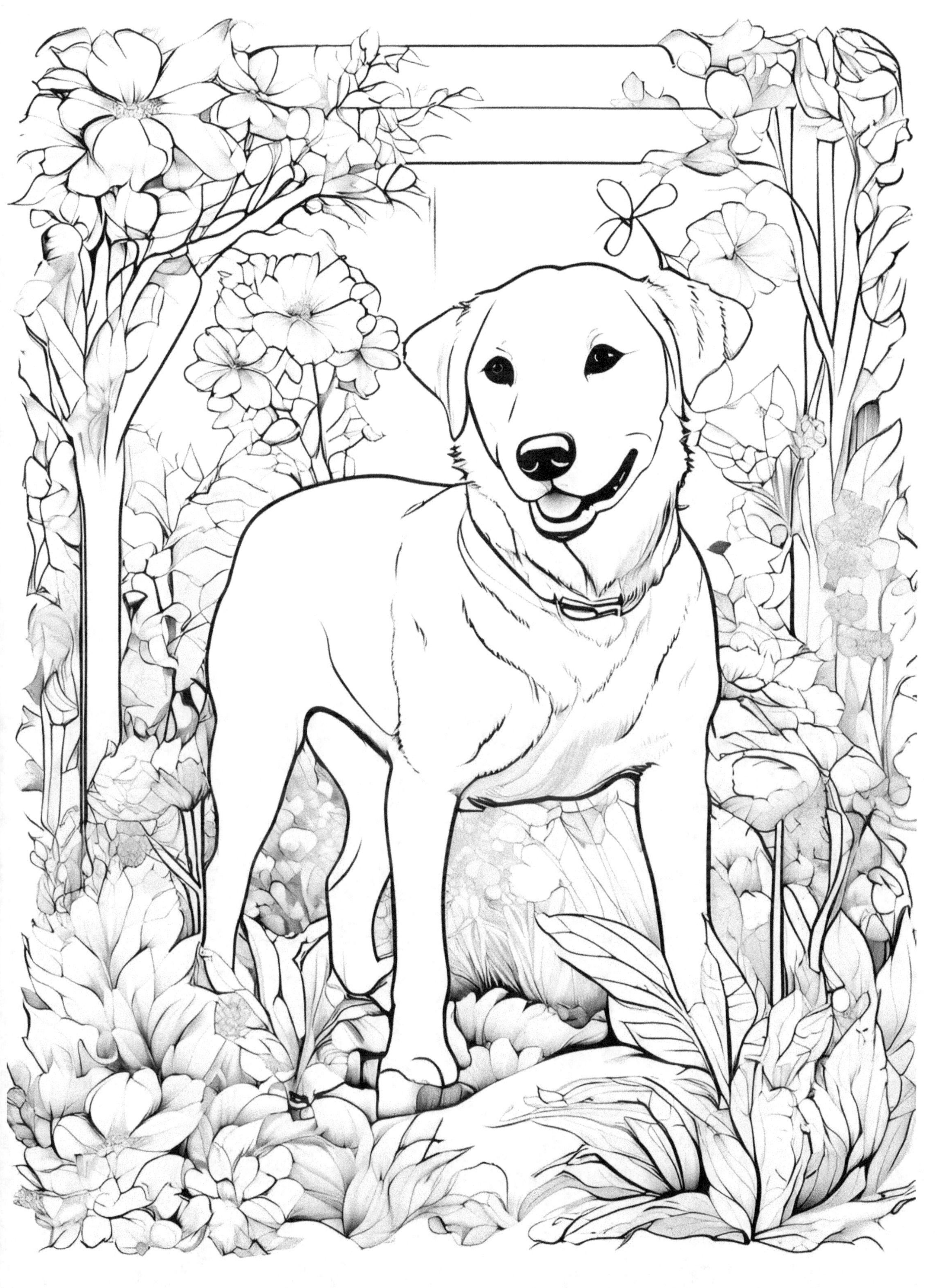

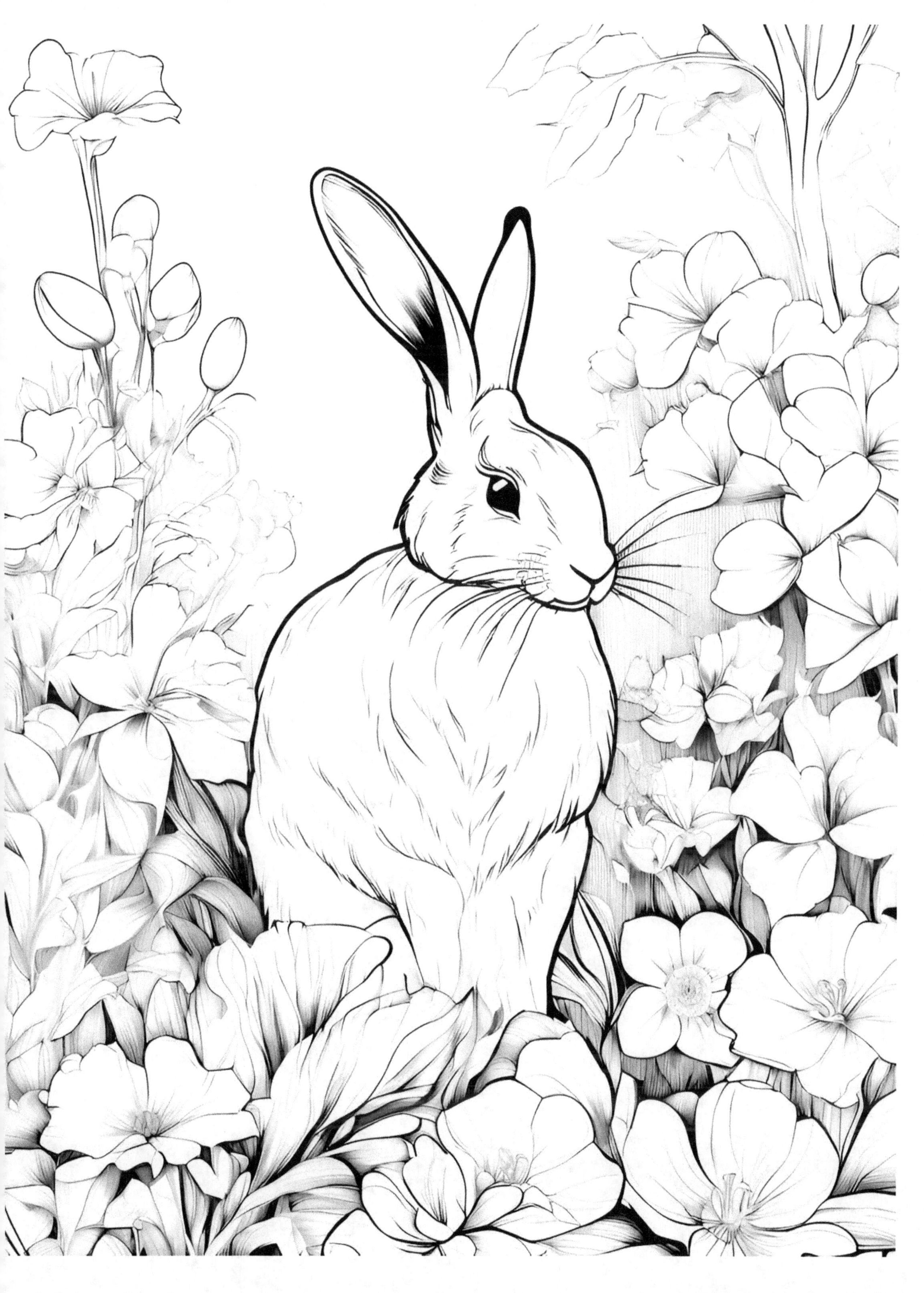

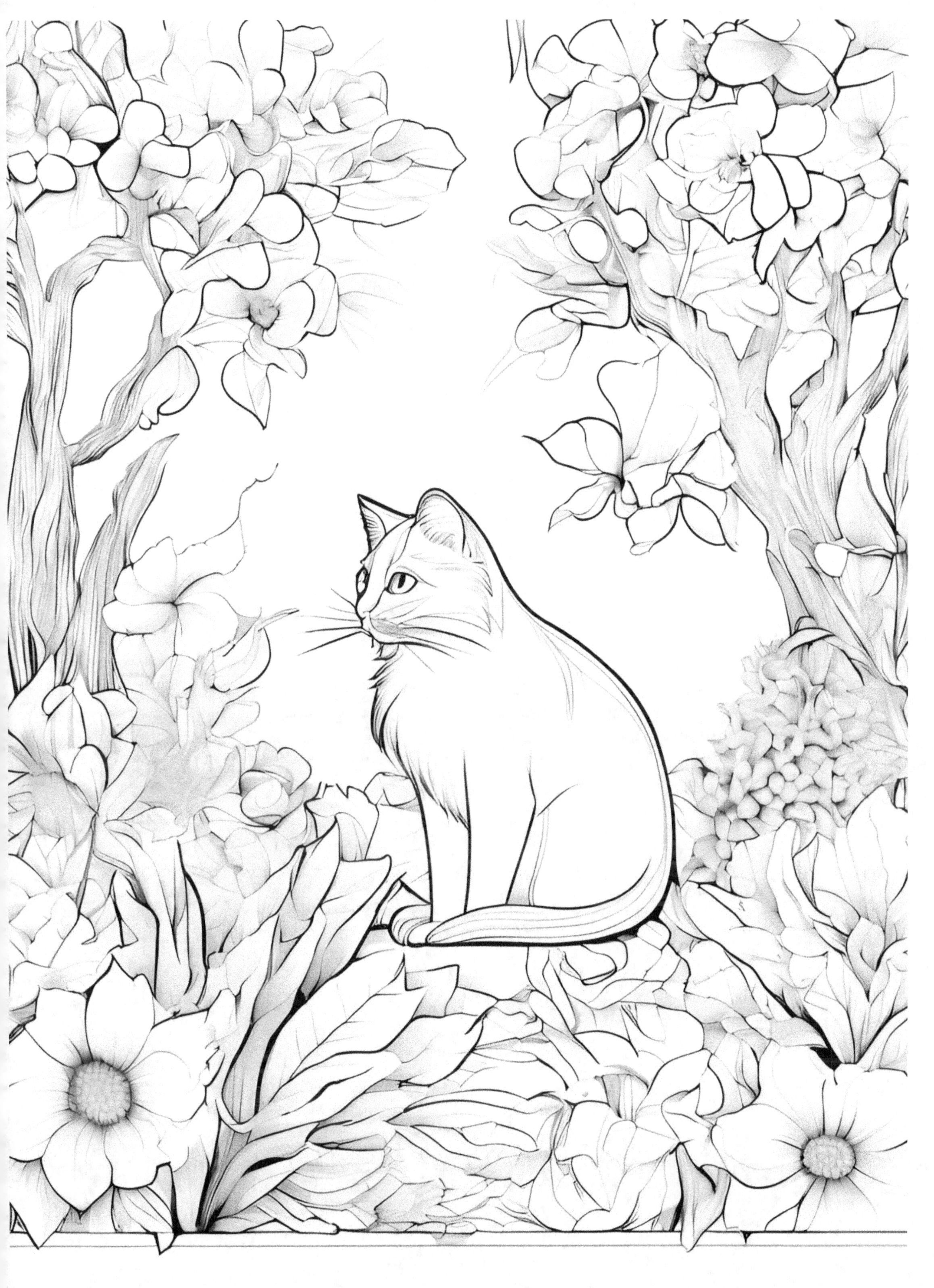

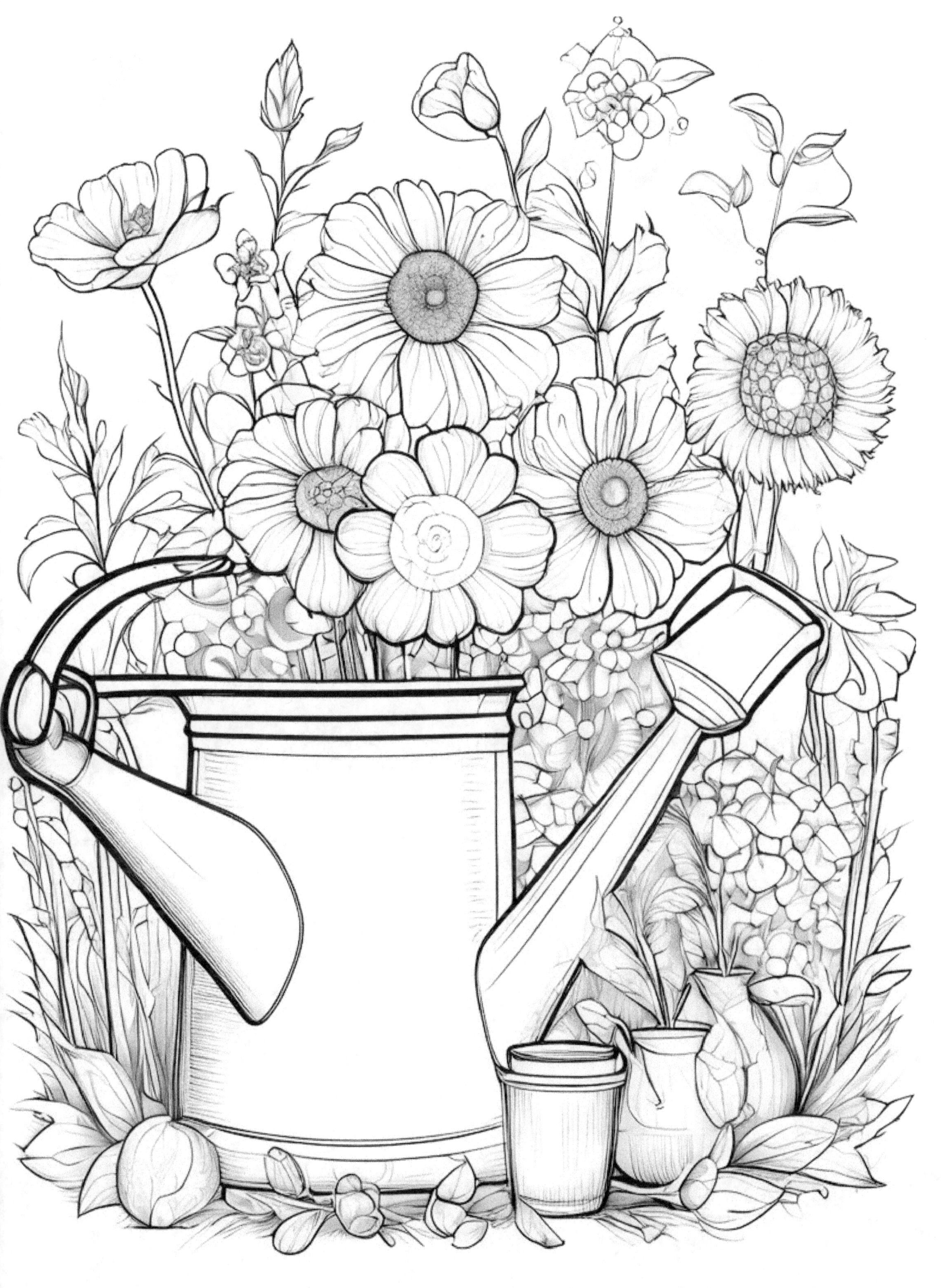

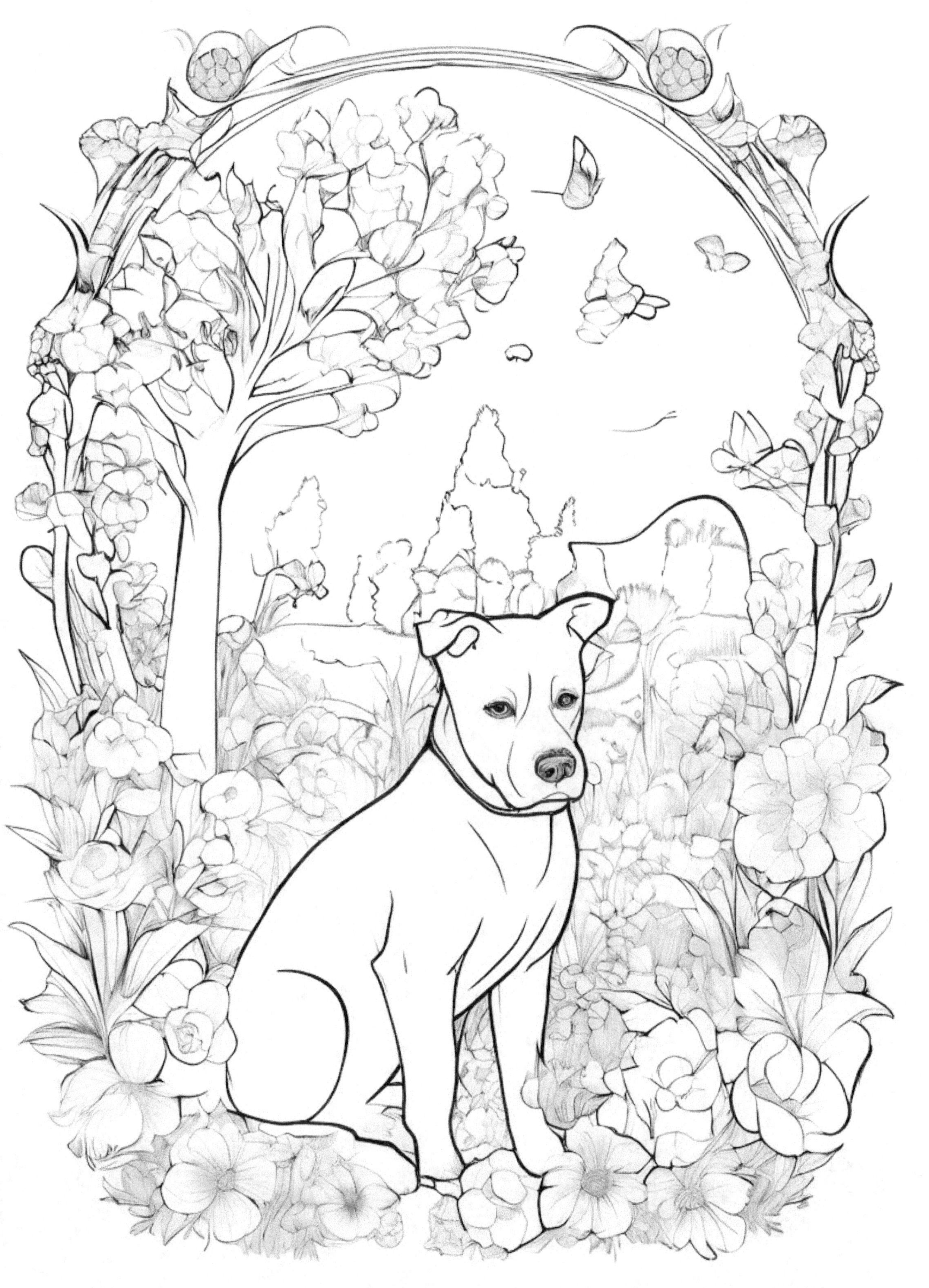

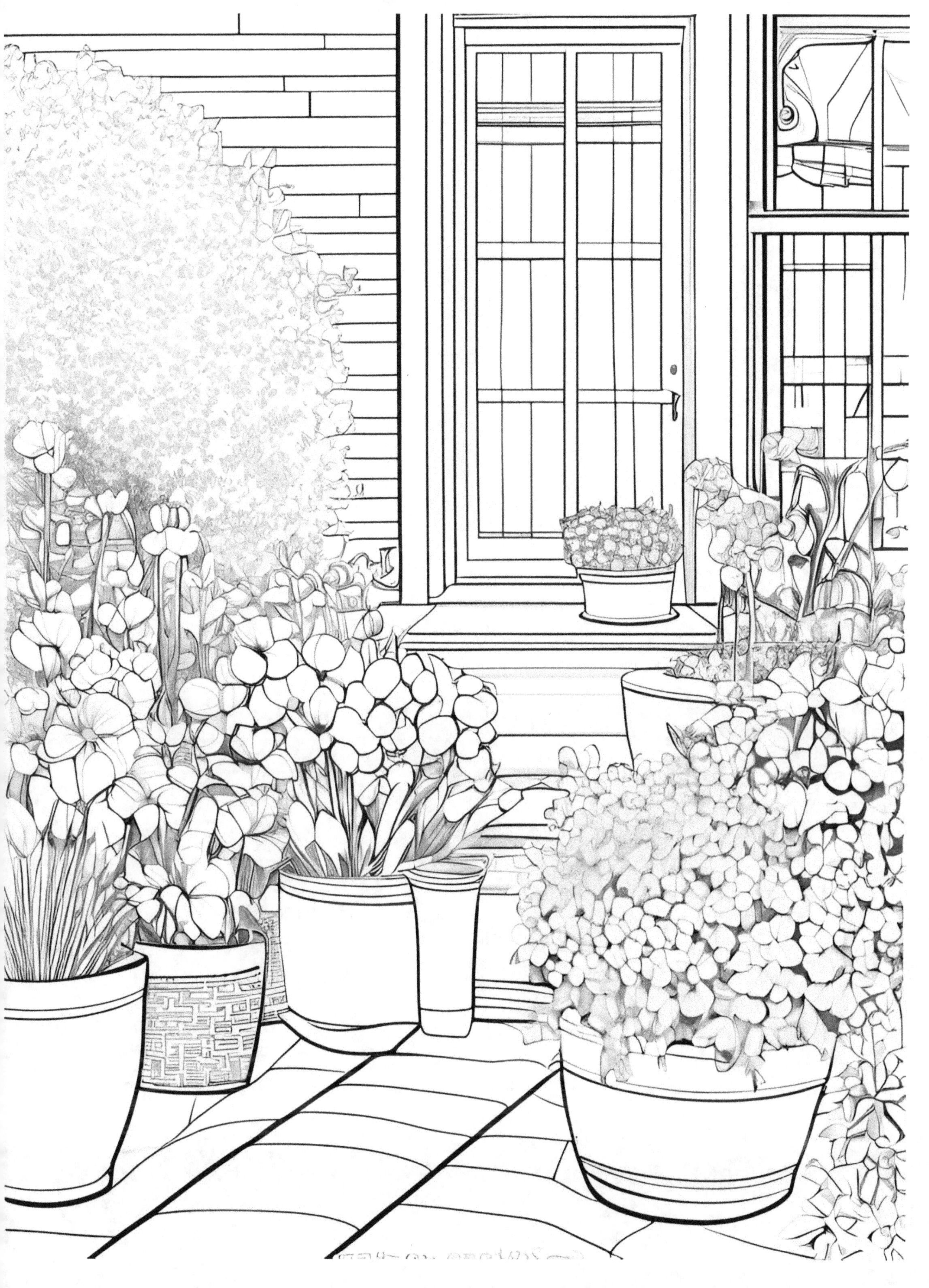

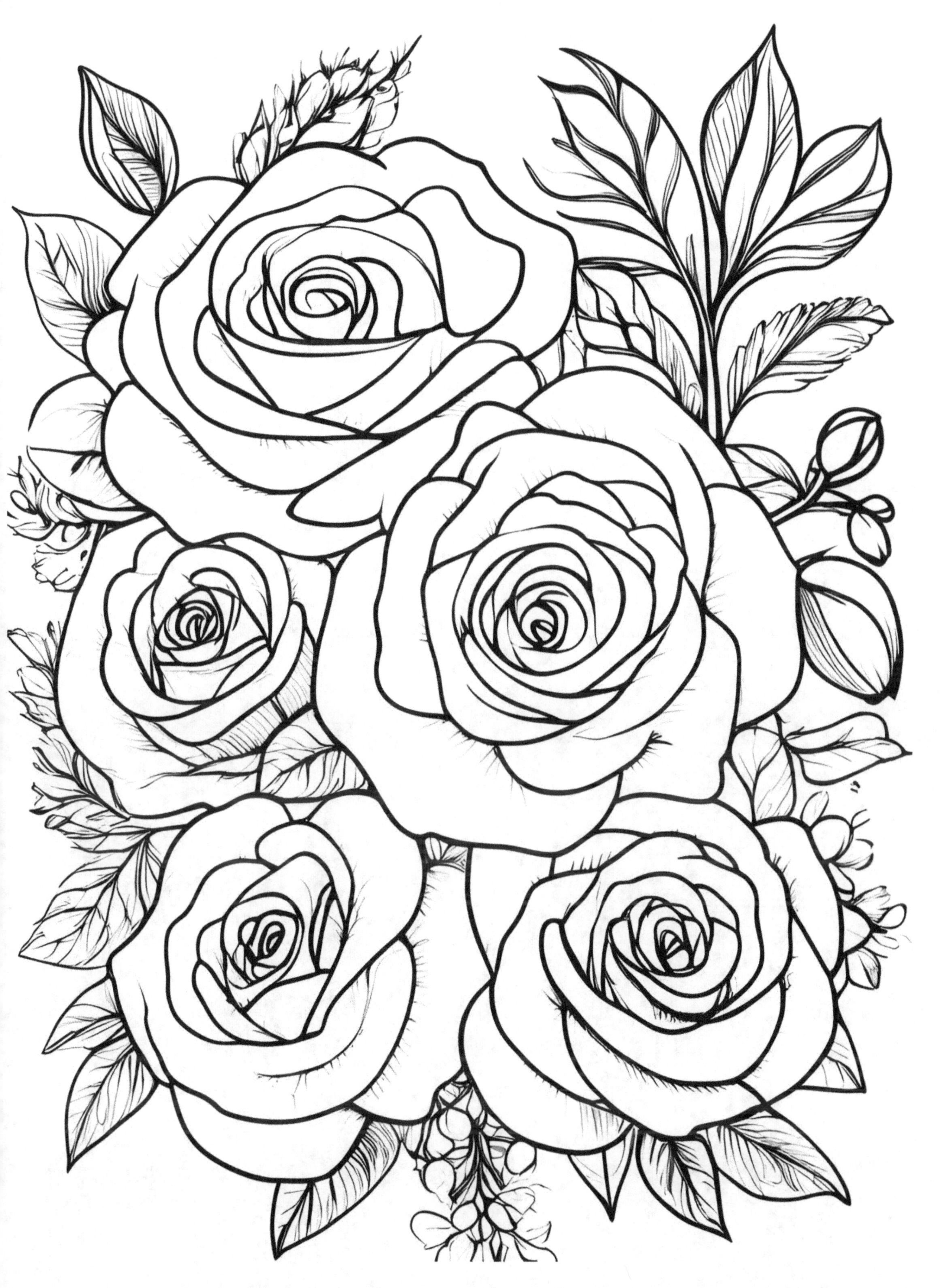

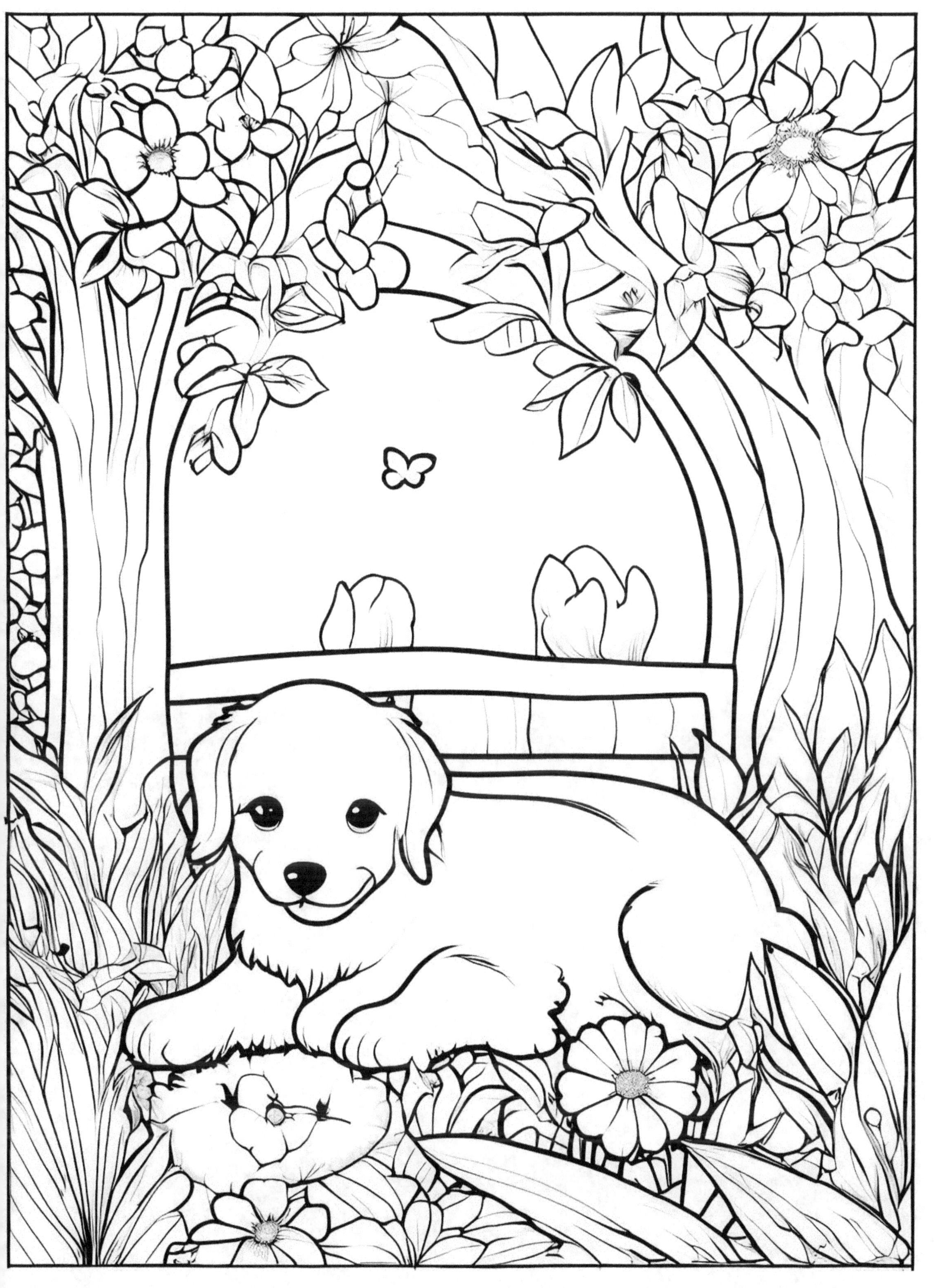

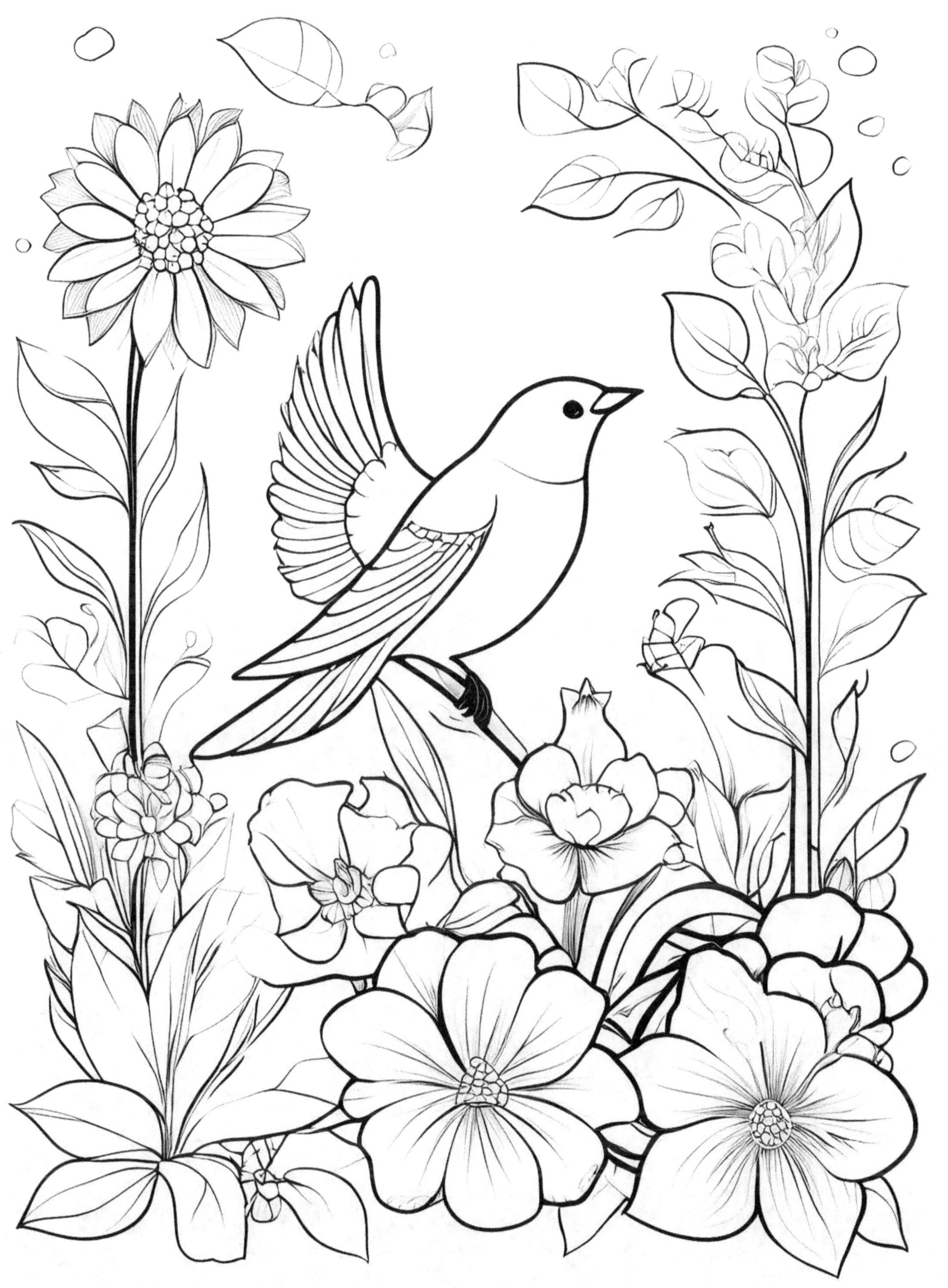

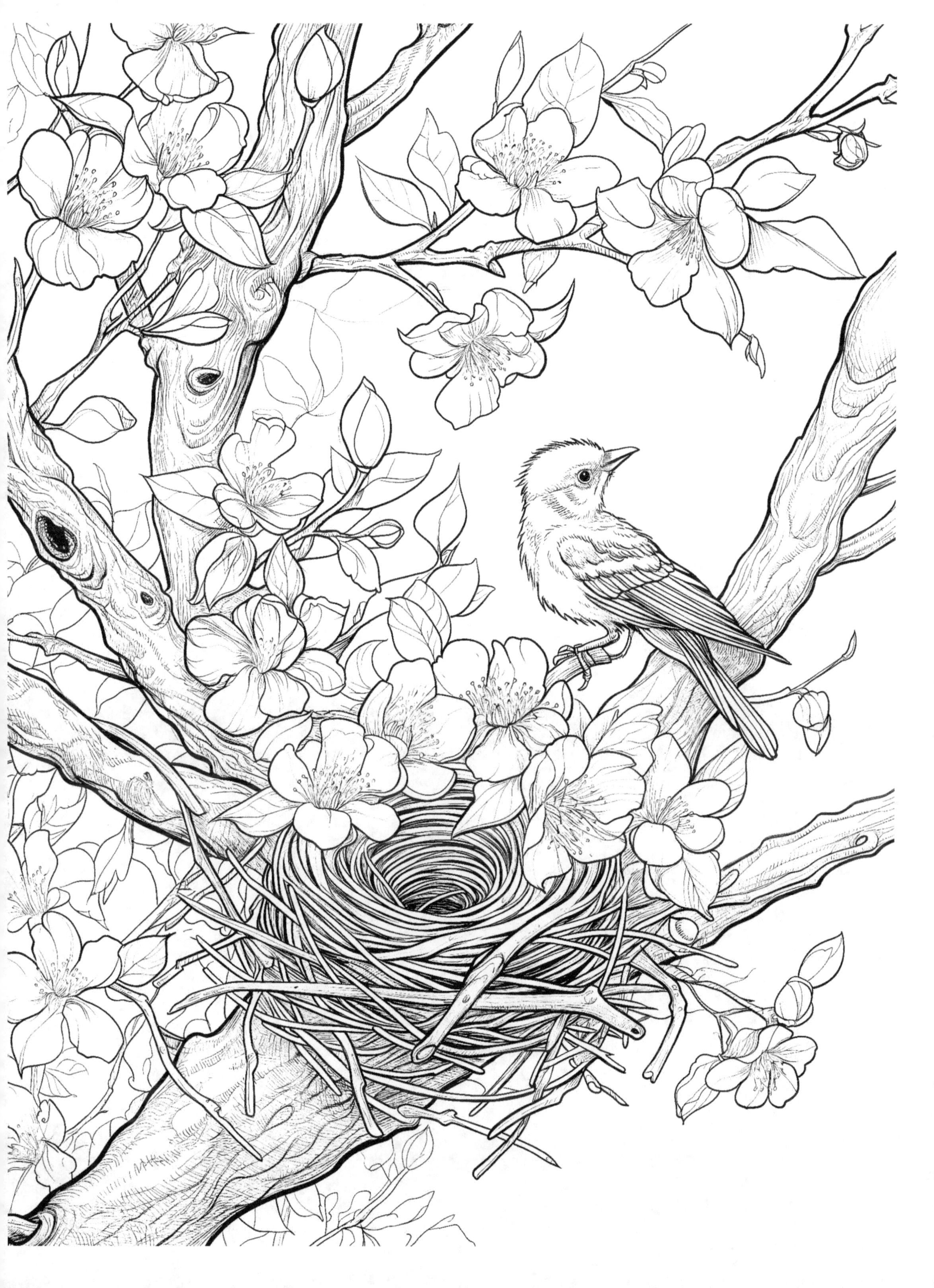

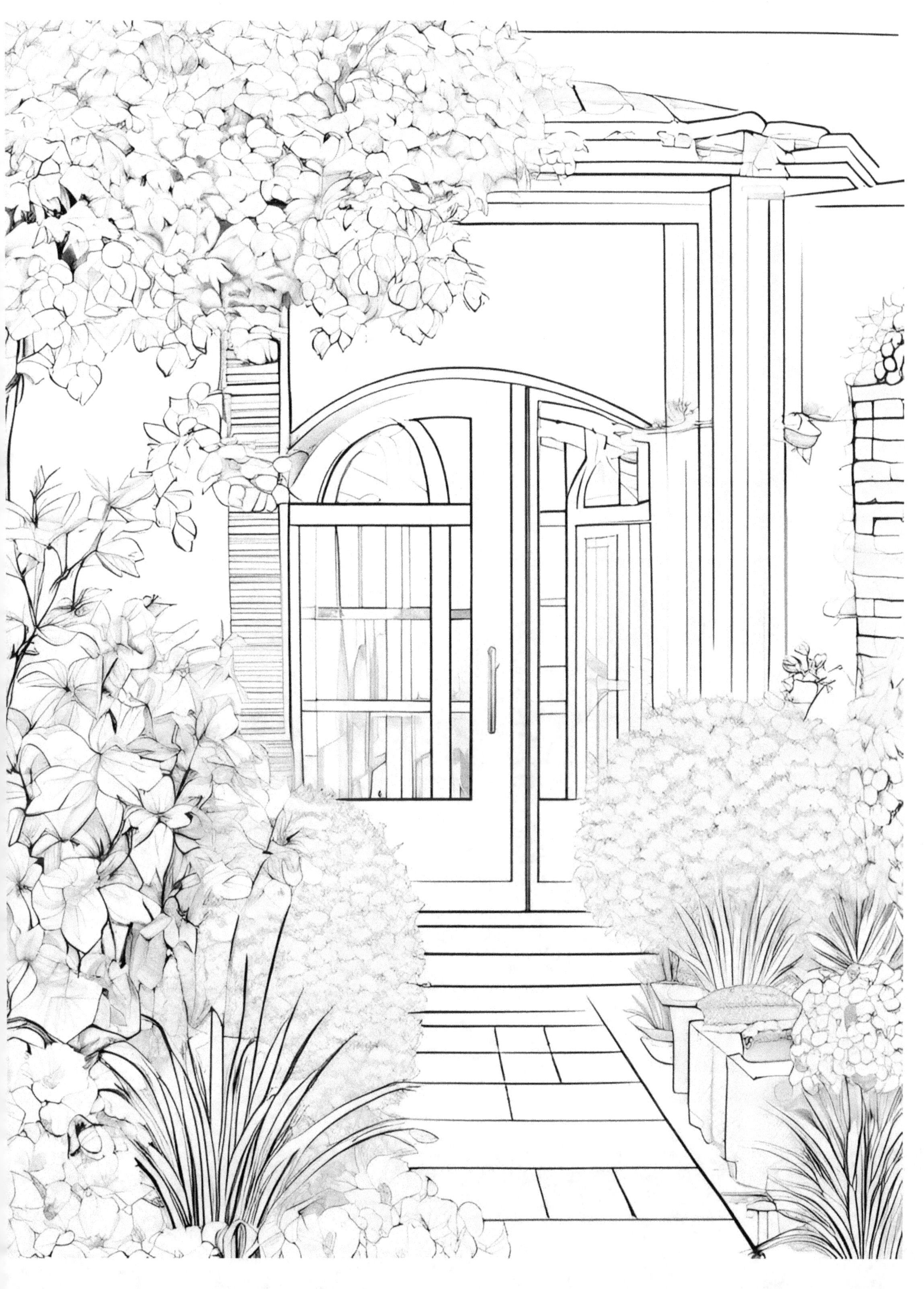

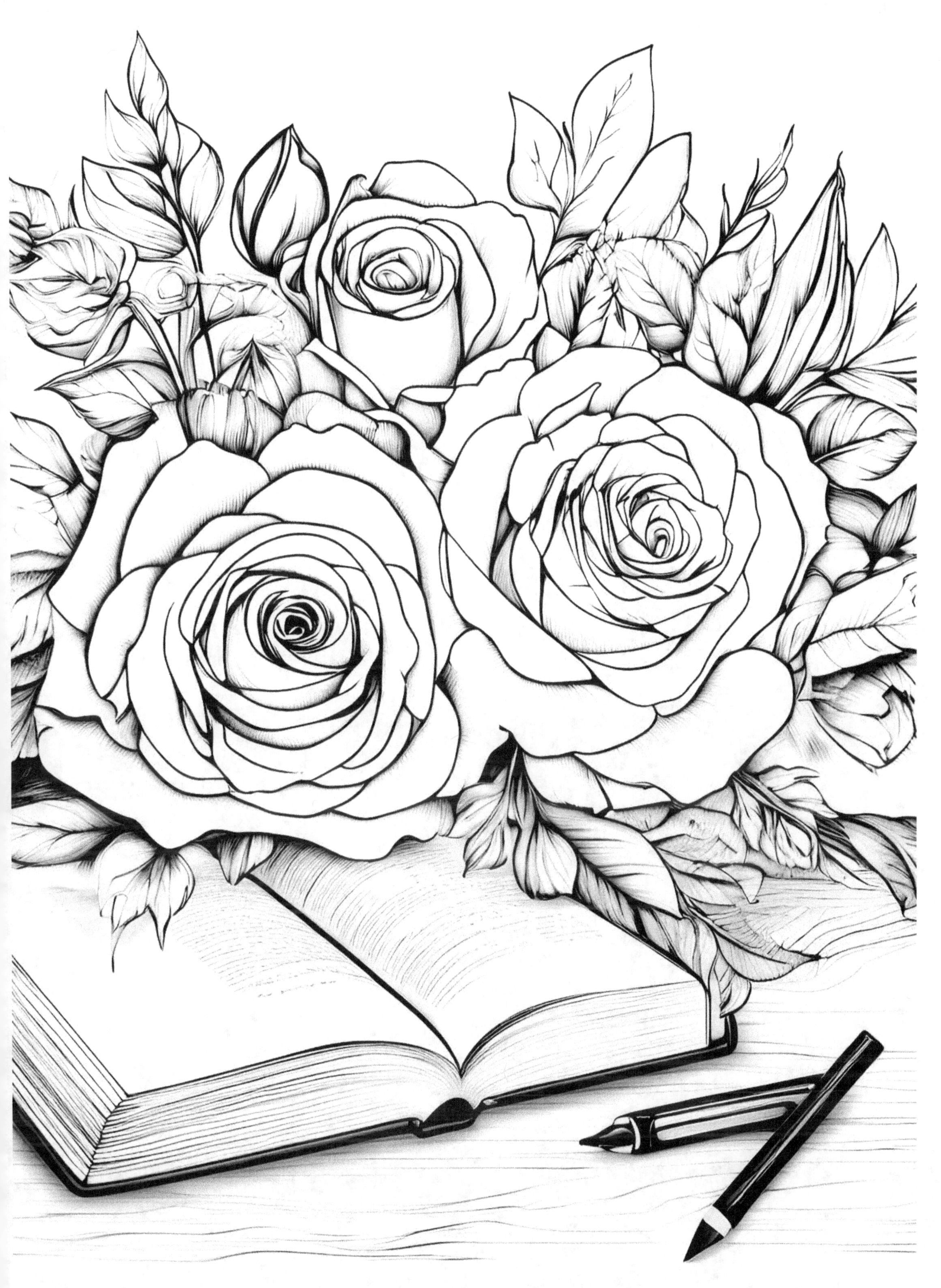

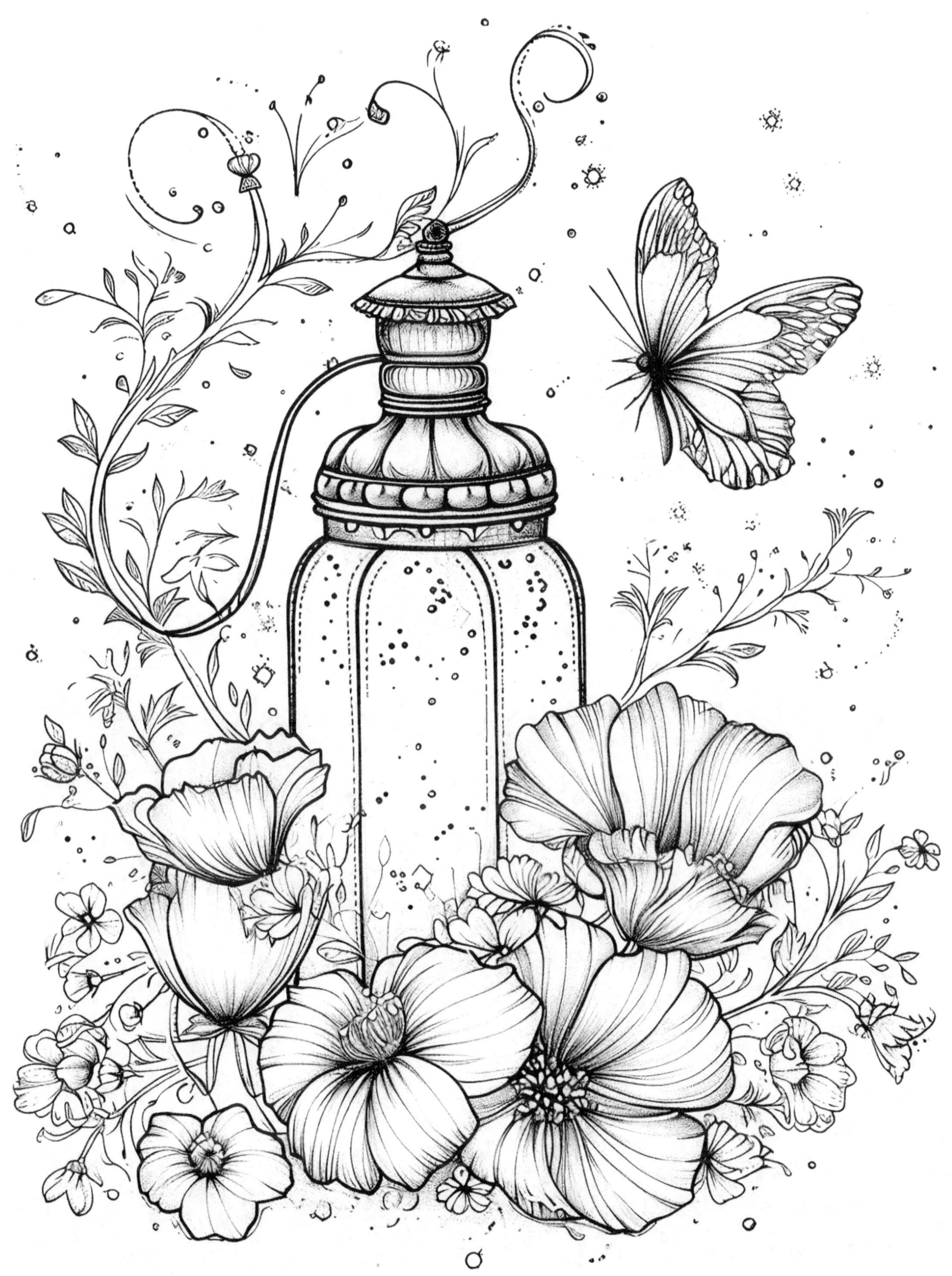

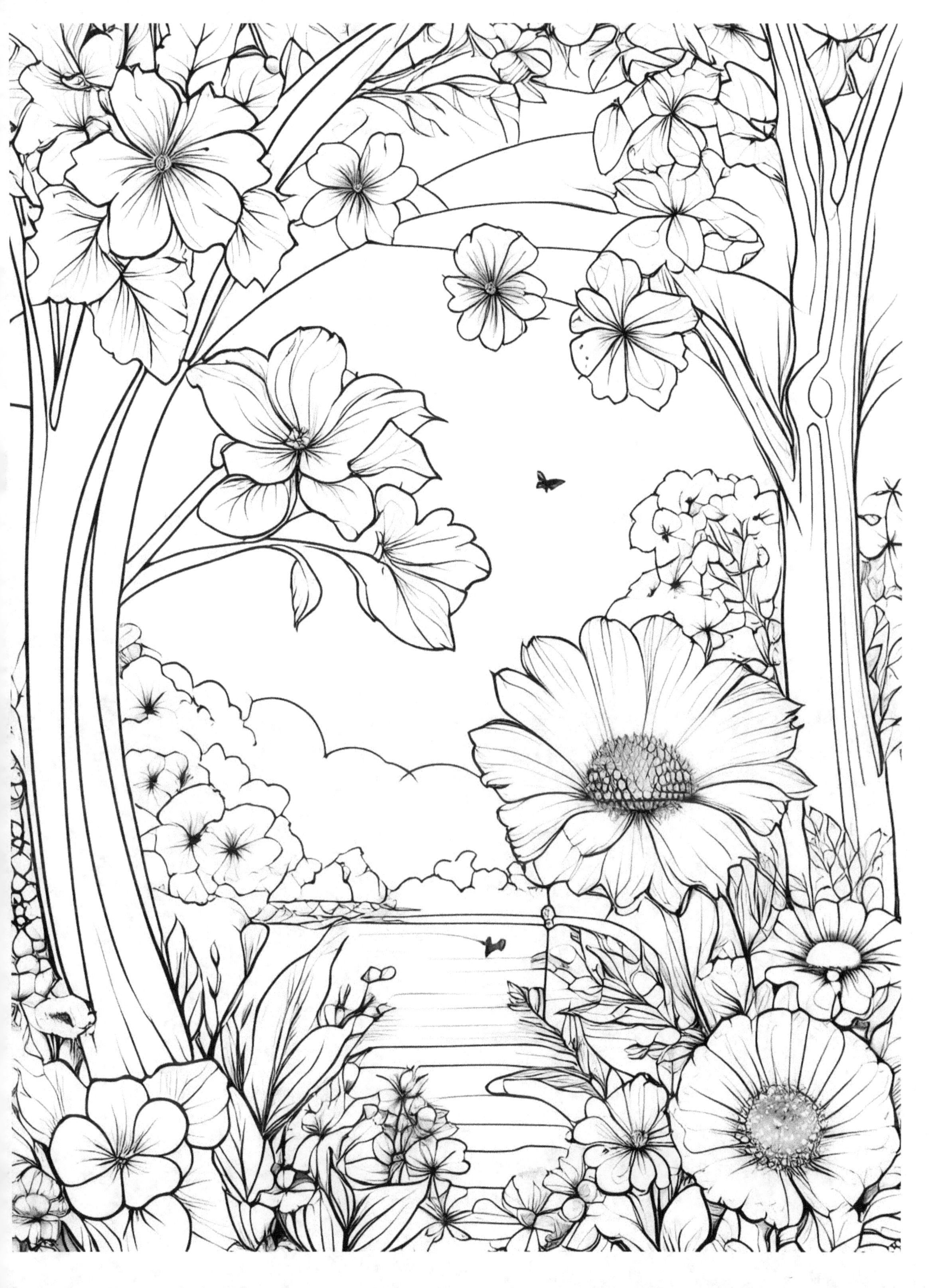

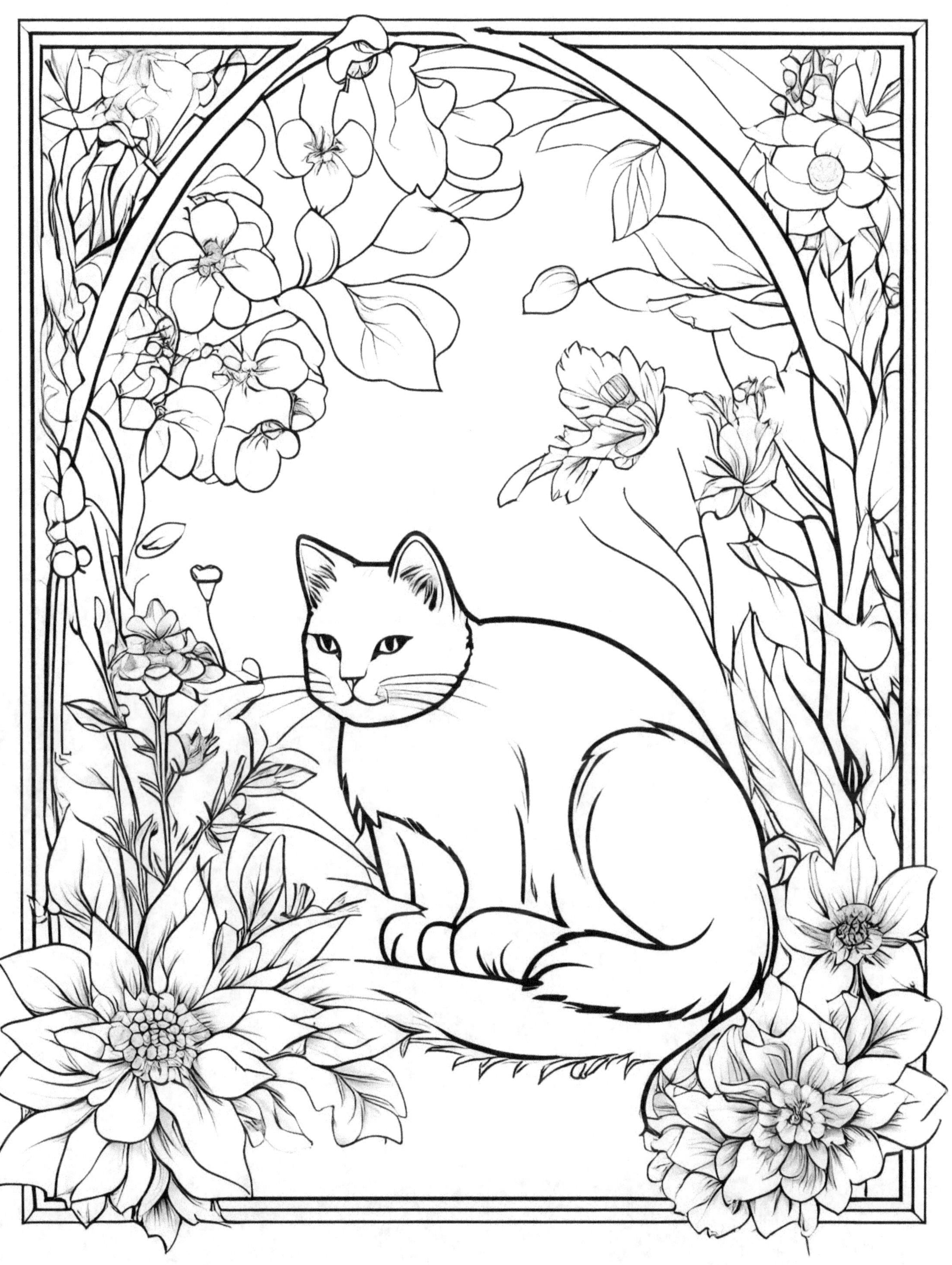

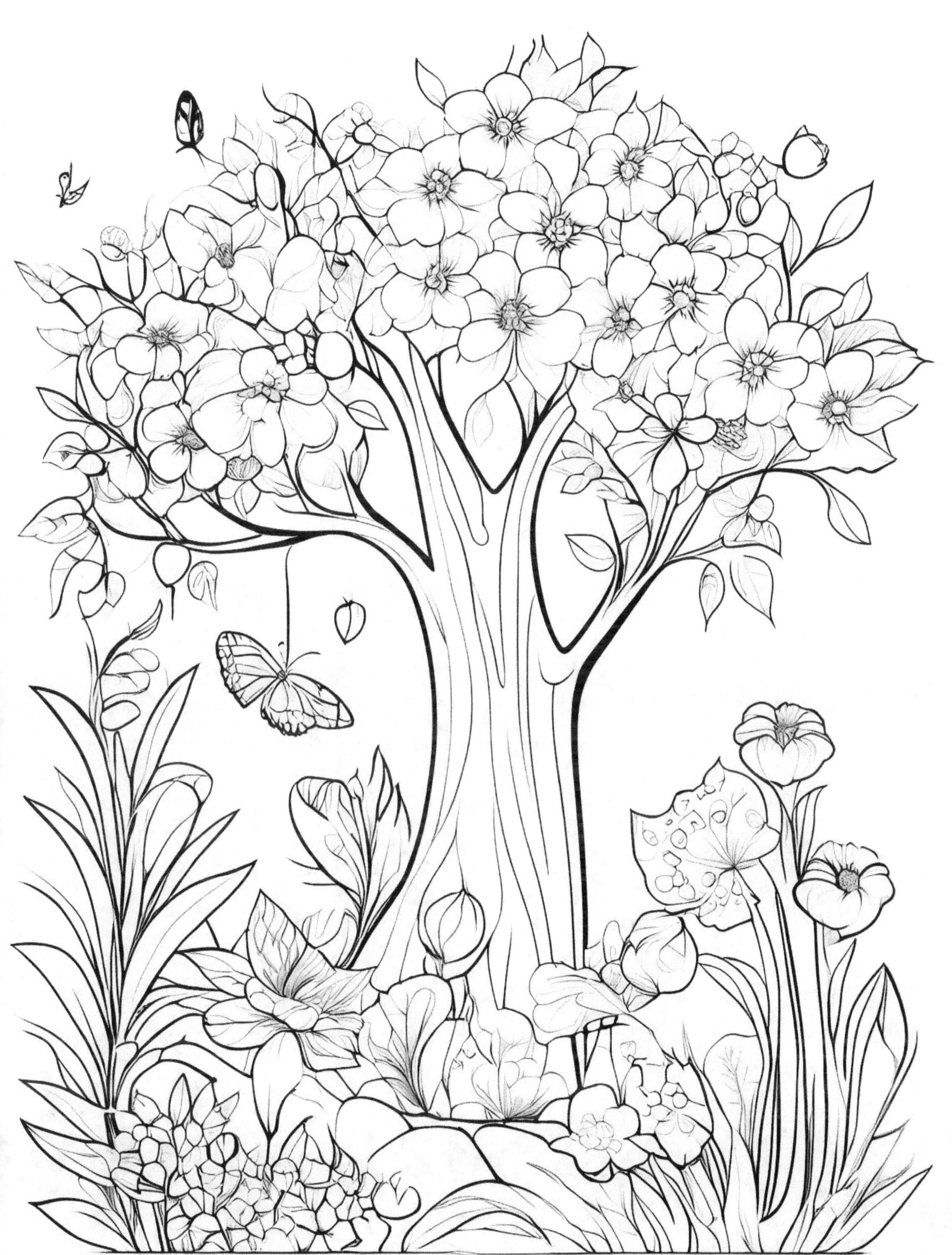